P9-DHF-708

F

Also by the Author

Use Both Sides of Your Brain
The Brain User's Guide

Make the Most of Your Mind

BY

Tony Buzan

A Fireside Book
Published by Simon & Schuster
New York London Toronto Sydney Tokyo Singapore

Fireside

Rockefeller Center
1230 Avenue of the Americas
New York, New York 10020

Text copyright © 1977, 1984 by Tony Buzan
Illustrations copyright © 1977, 1984 by Colt Books Limited

All right reserved
including the right of reproduction
in whole or in part in any form

First Fireside Edition, 1988

Originally published in Great Britain by Colt Books Limited.

FIRESIDE and colophon are registered trademarks
of Simon & Schuster Inc.

Designed by Irving Perkins and Associates
Manufactured in the United States of America

10 9 8 7

Library of Congress Cataloging in Publication Data
Buzan, Tony.
    Make the most of your mind.
    Bibliography: p.
    Includes index.
    1. Intellect.   2. Thought and thinking.   3. Brain.
4. Success.   I. Title.
BF431.B88   1984   153   83-22218
ISBN 0-671-49519-4 Pbk.

Acknowledgments

I would like to thank those people who have specially helped to make this book possible: Joseph Adams, Ken Adams, Mortimer Adler, Professor Zita Albes, Mrs. Bakhtiar, David Bolton, Mark Brown, Helga Buechner, John Bush, Joy Buttery, Barry Buzan, Gordon Buzan, Jean Buzan, Jeremy Cartland, Derek Chapman, Bill Chester, Gina Chester, Bernard Chibnall, Pan Collins, Paul Collins, Bernard Cowley, Keith Davis, Terry Dixon, Costas Florides, Lorraine Gill, Robert Heller, Harold Hemming, Moofy Hemming, Brian Helweg Larsen, Hermione Lovel, Alexander Luria, Joe McMahon, Anette McGee, John McNulty, Heinz Norden, Robert Ornstein, Anne Parks, Michael Ronan, Peter Russell, Robin Sales, John Staheli, Louisa Service, Caroline Shott, Chris Stevens, Aida Svendsen, Susan Thame, Nancy Thomas, Robert Thouless, Nicholas Wade, Bill Watts, Brian Wills, Linda and Robert Yeatman.

Contents

Make the
Most of Your
Mind

Introduction

Your Brain's Potential

Your brain is like a sleeping giant. During recent years, researches in psychology, education, biochemistry, physics, and mathematics have shown that the potential of your brain is far greater than was generally imagined. Even the commonly heard statement that on average we use only 1 percent of our brains may well be wrong because it now seems that we use even less than 1 percent—which means that an enormous amount of your capability is still available for development.

This book is designed to help you develop that astounding untapped potential. The first chapter outlines some of the most recent findings about your brain, including news from the most exciting "brain frontier": the different mental functions of the left and right sides of your brain. These discoveries and other facts about the structure of your brain and the number of connective patterns it can make are described in a way that will help you use the information to improve your own mental performance.

The next three chapters deal with memory and how you can improve your basic capacity as well as your special abilities for remembering facts, names, and faces; listening and how to select "keys" that help you to concentrate; and seeing, a chapter that concentrates on new findings about your eyes' ability to see more clearly, more analytically, more extensively—and faster. Your visual capacity is directly related to reading and speed reading. Diagrams show how your eyes normally function and how this function can be enormously improved, giving automatic increases in reading speed and efficiency.

The information from these early chapters is next applied to note-making and the creative organization of thought. Methods for reducing the volume of notes you make are outlined, and these are combined with other techniques to help you make note-making more effective. With this new note-making ability, creativity can also be enhanced. Techniques like "brain patterning" are included with examples and exercises that will help you to improve your own creative thinking.

The last two chapters give a simple introduction to two areas that often cause people mental stress: numbers and logic.

The numeracy chapter shows that everyone has a latent mathematical ability, regardless of what he or she may have been told, and outlines simple techniques for handling addition, subtraction, multiplication, and division more confidently. The chapter also includes some fast-calculating techniques that will enable you to perform mental gymnastics in your head within seconds, while others spend minutes with pencil and paper.

The final chapter is on logic and analysis. It outlines, with examples, ten basic areas of logical thinking in which you can improve your ability to analyze, to make judgments, and to present your own thoughts clearly.

SELF-CHECK 1—What Were You Taught?

In your formal schooling you were no doubt taught a wide range of academic subjects. Most people find that despite this they were taught very little about how they and their minds work. The following "Yes/ No" questions will give you an idea of what you may have missed. Record your answers as you go along.

In your formal education were you taught about:

1. the major left/right divisions of your brain?

Yes/ No

2. the general structure of your brain and its brain cells?

Yes/ No

3. the mathematical, memory, and learning potential of your brain?

Yes/ No

4. the way your memory changes during learning?

Yes/ No

5. the way your memory changes after learning?

Yes/ No

6. special memory systems for improving all kinds of recall?

Yes/ No

7. how to improve your listening ability?

Yes/ No

8. the way in which your eyes move when they take in information?

Yes/ No

9. the way in which eyes can be taught to take in more information than they normally do?

Yes/ No

10. how visual guides can increase your reading speed?

Yes/ No

11. the nature of comprehension and how this can be improved?

Yes/ No

12. shorthand techniques?

Yes/ No

13. the way in which words and images "work" in your mind?

Yes/ No

14. note-making techniques allowing you to form "mental pictures" of your thoughts?

Yes/ No

15. how to prepare completely for, and write, examinations?

Yes/ No

16. how to plan and present reports, speeches and presentations?

Yes/ No

17. the meaning of creativity?

Yes/ No

18. the potential of the average brain's creativity?

Yes/ No

19. special techniques for vastly speeding up addition, subtraction, multiplication, and division?

Yes/ No

20. techniques for analyzing arguments in order to enable you to pick out the logical flaws?

Yes/ No

Most people answer "Yes" to only a very few of these questions. Many answer "Yes" to none of them. One of the purposes of this book is to correct this imbalance.

Developing Your Approach

Some readers may wish to make a major project of improving themselves and may decide to devote considerable time and effort to the project. Others may wish to turn to this book for occasional help in areas where they need special attention.

Both approaches are completely valid, and can be compared with approaches to sports. If you wish to become a champion, complete dedication is necessary, with daily work and practice. If you wish to become an adequate "social" tennis player, basic information is required, plus occasional attention to footwork, angle of the racket, smoothness of strokes; such small adjustments can make major differences in performance. It is the same with your brain. Even a slight adjustment to the way in which you use your brain can produce dramatic results.

Whether you use *Make the Most of Your Mind* in order to excel or to improve your general mental performance, the book will give you a new self-awareness and confidence whenever you have to use your ability to think.

Chapter Design

Each chapter is constructed to make it easy for you to scan, read, and remember. At the beginning of each chapter is a brief summary of the contents. After each summary is an even shorter "key word" summary which extracts the main idea words from the chapter. Included in most of the chapters are games and tests that will enable you to judge and analyze your own performance. In many of these games and tests there is no scoring at all. In those items which are scored, the score is judged neither "bad" nor "good"; it simply serves as a baseline from which you are able to improve, no matter where you start.

Further Reading

At the very end of the book is a list of recommended books for further reading. This is divided into three sections: psychology/practical, general reading, and novels. These books, whether they are more academic or more entertaining, will provide you with additional information about your brain, as well as with much food for further thought.

General Advice

When reading this or most other books, it is advisable to scan the book before settling down to an "in-depth" reading. As one reader put it: "Case the joint before going in and getting what you want!" You will find that scanning enables you to get a more complete grasp of the entire subject, making in-depth reading that much easier.

It is advisable to skip any difficult areas, then go back to them at a later stage, when the additional information that you have gathered from the rest of the book will make the difficult areas easier to understand.

Developing Your Potential

Why is so little of the brain's potential ability used?

One of the main reasons is that until only recently we have known very little about the brain and the way it works. Many of the problems we encounter in the use of our mental abilities do not result from any lack in the brain's basic capacity but from inadequate knowledge of its potential and how to use it. Our increasing understanding of the structure of the brain and the way it functions can help us to overcome both this difficulty and the lack of confidence so many of us experience in making the most of the ability we already possess.

SELF-CHECK 2—Your Problems

On a separate sheet of paper note down, *in detail*, all the problems you have in using your brain. Make sure that you are honest with yourself and that you leave nothing out. The more you bring the problems to light, the easier it will be for you to solve them as you progress through the book.

The Problems*

No matter how many you wrote down, don't worry. Although your own list and the following list of other people's problems might seem a little forbidding, there is still hope, for the brain is capable of performing more than adequately, even when we place it under the pressures that give rise to many of these problems.

* The problems listed here are a summary of the problems given by people attending Tony Buzan's courses. They include businessmen, university students, housewives, children, politicians, teachers, and professors. No matter what walk of life the people came from, the pattern of their problems was very similar. Most of these problems were significantly reduced when they were able to apply to the problems the basic information about their brains which is outlined in the following chapters.

What the lists signify is that we have not really been given enough information about how our brains work. Most of us can be compared to the unfortunate owner of a Rolls-Royce who, not knowing how the machine operates, mistakenly lubricates it with water, and then blames it for not working.

Recently, so much new light has been shed on the structure of your brain that we now *know* it can be helped to function far more effectively. The Rolls-Royce does work, and there are better ways of lubricating its ability.

age	discipline	languages
aims	distraction	layout
alertness	dyslexia	laziness
amount	education	learning
analogies	ego	lighting
analysis	emotions	listening
anxiety	environment	logic
appreciation	expression	meetings
aptitude	fatigue	memory
assessment	fear	mental blocks
assimilation	feedback	mental set
association	fitness	methodology
atmosphere	flexibility	mislinking
attention	fluency	motivation
attitude	frustration	nerves
back-skipping	getting down to it	noise
bias	goals	note-taking
biorhythms	goal-setting	numbers
boredom	health	objectives
clarity	hierarchies	objectivity
classifying	humor	ordering
comfort	imagery	organization
communication	imagination	panic
complication	impatience	perception
conflict	inhibition	persuasion
confidence	initiation	planning
content	intelligence	prejudice
continuity	interest	preparation
conversation	interpretation	presentation
credibility	interrogation	pressure
decisiveness	interviewing	priorities
definition	intuition	problem-solving
dictation	irrelevance	rapport

rationalization
reading
reassembling
recalling
regression
rejection
relaxation
retention
reviewing
rhythm
scanning
selection
sequencing

skipping
sleep
speaking
speed
spelling
stickability
stopping
stress
study-reading
style
subvocalization
temperature
tension

thinking ahead/back
time
typography
uncertainty
understanding
verbosity
vision
visualizing
vocabulary
vocalization
willpower
writing

Your Brain

What is the real potential of your brain, and what is its physical nature? In this chapter the early history of thought on the brain is briefly introduced, and then the latest and most significant findings about your brain are described: the left and right sides of your brain; the physical structure and connection patterns of your individual brain cells; the relationship between your upper and lower brain; and the number of electrochemical interactions continually taking place in your brain. The last section of the chapter discusses the question of mental ability in relation to age and suggests that you can teach an old dog new tricks.

KEY WORD SUMMARY

History-brain
Left and right sides
Brain cells
Brain connections
Electrochemical interactions
Your potential
Improving with age

From Past to Present

Did you know that your brain is divided into two halves? And furthermore, did you know that those two halves are two separate brains?

As little as two thousand years ago mankind knew virtually nothing about the brain. Before the Greeks, the mind was not even considered to be part of the human body but was thought to exist as some form of vapor, gas, or disembodied spirit.

Surprisingly, the Greeks did not get us that much further, and even Aristotle, their most famous philosophical thinker and the founder of modern science, concluded after extensive investigations that the center of sensation and memory was located in the heart. From the time of the Greeks to the beginning of the Renaissance there was virtually no progress at all. During the Renaissance, a period of great intellectual awakening, it was finally realized that the center of thought and consciousness was located in the head, but the brain remained a mystery.

It was not until the twentieth century that the really great strides forward were made in our understanding of our own brains, and many people still assume that it was in the first half of the century that the greatest advances were made. On the contrary, through the 1930s and 1940s we still believed the brain to be a simple machine, operating much like the very first computers, in which a few basic messages went in and were placed in the appropriate boxes, and that that was all there was to it. This model of the brain was common in first-year psychology and educational textbooks until the late 1950s.

It was not until very recently that the really major breakthroughs were made. These developments are so significant that they are already changing the foundations of psychology and education, and are emphasizing a fact sensed by many but until now impossible to "prove": that the average brain is far more capable than we ever believed.

A number of new findings stand out as particularly significant.

Your Left and Right Brain

For some time it has been known that the brain is divided into two sides, left and right. It has also been known that if damage is done to the left side of the brain, the right side of the body tends to become paralyzed, and, correspondingly, that if damage is done to the right side of the brain, the left side of the body tends to become paralyzed. In other words, each side of your brain controls the opposite side of your body.

The recent research of Professor Robert Ornstein of the University of California has thrown more light on the different activities handled by each side of the brain.

Starting with the realization that the two halves of the brain are biologically similar and can more realistically be thought of as two identical brains working in harmony, rather than as one brain divided into two, Professor Ornstein decided to find out if each of our separate brains handles different intellectual activities in addition to the different physical activities.

Placing special caps for measuring brain waves on some of his students, he asked them to do different kinds of mental tasks. They were asked to add lists of numbers, write formal letters and essays, arrange colored blocks, analyze logically, and think "daydreamy" thoughts. All the time these activities were being performed, Professor Ornstein was measuring the brain waves coming from the two halves of each person's brain.

His findings were both surprising and significant. In general the left brain handles the following mental activities:

1. mathematics
2. language
3. logic
4. analysis
5. writing
6. and other similar activities

and the right side of the brain handles very different activities:

1. imagination
2. color
3. music
4. rhythm
5. daydreaming
6. and other similar activities

Ornstein also found that people who had been trained to use one side of their brain more or less exclusively were relatively unable to use the other side, both in general and in those special situations where the activities specifically related to the other side were particularly needed.

Even more significant, Ornstein found that when the "weaker" of the two brains was stimulated and encouraged to work in cooperation with the stronger side, the end result was a great increase in overall ability and effectiveness.

These increases were larger than Ornstein anticipated: he had expected that by encouraging the weaker side to work in conjunction with the stronger side, he would get an increase of the type: 1 side + 1 side = twice as effective a performance. The actual result showed that the brain can sometimes work in a way different from the standard mathematics, for when one side was "added" to the other side, the result was often five to ten times more effectiveness.

Ornstein's findings have special significance for those of us educated in the West, for most of us have been trained in the three Rs: reading, writing, and arithmetic—left-brain, left-brain, left-brain. We have traditionally considered the student who is artistically talented, musical, good with his hands, and a bit "dreamy" to be unintelligent, stupid, nonuniversity material, and "thick." All the evidence now suggests that this has been a mistake, and that the more creative or artistic person is just as "intelligent" as the more academic person.

The Artist and the Scientist   This work has been further supported by an investigation into those people normally considered to be great artists and scientists. Einstein, for instance, often considered to be the greatest scientist of his time, was not simply a fuzzy-headed mathematical physicist whose brain was full of numbers and formulae. Records show that he failed mathematics at school and that he was nearly thrown out of college for daydreaming.

According to Einstein himself, he discovered his theory of relativity not seated in front of his desk, but while lying on a hill one summer day.

As he looked up with half-closed eyes, the sun dappled through his eyelashes, breaking into thousands of tiny sunbeams. Einstein won-

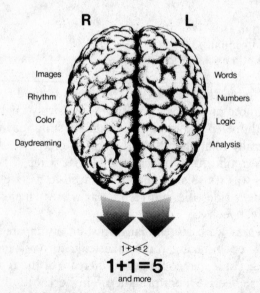

Your brain is divided into two separate brains. The left brain takes as its domain the following mental activities: words, numbers, logic and analysis. The right brain takes as its domain: images, color, daydreaming, etc. You have both "scientific" *and* "artistic" abilities.

dered what it would be like to go for a ride on one of those sunbeams, and in his imagination took himself on a journey through the universe. His imagination took him to a place where his formal training in physics told him he should not be. Concerned about this, he went back to his blackboard, and believing his imagination to be more correct than his formal training, worked out a new mathematics to explain the truth of what his brain had told him. Looking back, we can see that he was actually using both sides of his brain to an exceptional degree, the right side of his brain producing the beautiful imagined journey, and the left side of his brain being used to develop the new physics and mathematics, and to provide a formal framework for the image he had created. This combination provided mankind with one of the most significant theories of all time.

Similarly, studies of great artists have shown that they were not slap-happy splashers of color on canvas. Investigation of the notebooks of such famous painters as Klee, Cézanne, and Picasso have shown them to be exceptionally mathematical and geometrical in their descriptions of what they were trying to do, outlining in intricate detail the specific interrelationships they were trying to make with color, form and line. Again and again investigation shows that the great minds have been mistakenly labeled either "artistic" or "scientific" when in fact they were both.

Perhaps the best example of this is the man considered by many to have had one of the greatest brains of all time: Leonardo da Vinci. Leonardo's renown as history's most complete man is based on the very fact that he excelled in his mathematical, linguistic, logical, and analytical faculties, while also excelling in his ability to use imagination, color, rhythm, and form.

The intelligent conclusion to be drawn from Ornstein's work is that each one of us is potentially both exceptionally scientific and exceptionally artistic. If we are at the moment lopsided it is not because of an inherent disability, but simply because one side of our brain has not been given as much opportunity to develop as the other.

The Structure of Your Brain—Your Brain Cells

The second new and significant piece of information about our brains was discovered by Professor Pyotr Anokhin, the protégé and direct descendant of Pavlov in psychology.

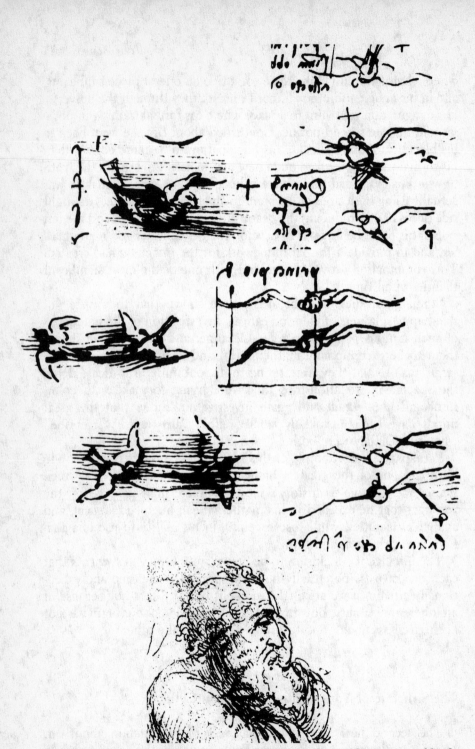

Leonardo da Vinci's visual acuity enabled him to freeze the motion of birds in flight to the exactness of a camera. These drawings demonstrate his analysis of the mechanics of birds' flight.

For centuries, the brain had been considered as merely a three-and-a-half-pound lump of gray matter. With the development of the microscope it was discovered that the brain's crumpled outer layer was far more complex than had previously been believed, and that it was composed of many thousands of intricate nerve and blood pathways.

As microscopy continued to improve, so did our knowledge of the structure of the brain. It was soon realized that each brain was composed of millions of tiny cells called neurons. In a scientific saga similar to that of astronomy—in which more has been discovered the more powerful our measuring instruments have become—scientists next discovered that each brain cell was like a tiny octopus, having a center, or nucleus, and a large number of little tentacles radiating in all directions from it.

Continuing on their magnification journey, the scientists found that each of these tentacles had thousands of tiny protuberances, much like the suction pads on the tentacles of the octopus, but protruding from all sides of the tentacle.

By this stage in the investigation they had calculated that the average brain contained a truly staggering number of individual neurons: 10,000,000,000!

Scientists have discovered that each brain contains 10,000,000,000 brain cells. Each one of these cells is like a tiny octopus, with many connection points on each of the many arms.

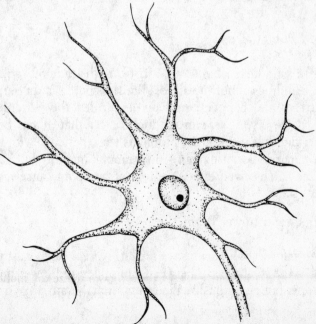

It was thought for a while that the number of brain cells determined the comparative intelligence of the person, but this belief was soon laid to rest when it was found that many people with "large" brains had been apparently unintelligent, whereas a number of people with "small" brains had shown considerable intelligence.

Connections and Pathways in Your Brain

Professor Anokhin was among the first to realize that it was not the number of brain cells that determined intelligence but something to do with the little protuberances on the brain cells' tentacles. He found that each protuberance was connected to at least one other, and by means of electrochemical impulses these two could form little patterns with other individuals and other groups. As he progressed, Anokhin realized that each brain was a fantastic interlinking of patterns formed by the thousands of protuberances on the many arms of the many millions of brain cells.

In the last year of his life, Professor Anokhin calculated the number of connections and pathways that could be made by a normal brain. He emphasized, as a scientist, that his estimate was conservative, and concluded his last public statement by saying he was convinced that no man was alive or had ever lived who even approached the full use of his brain. The number he calculated is still staggering scientists and teachers alike: 1 followed by 10,000,000 kilometers of standard typewritten zeros!

Unlimited Potential?

Ornstein's findings about our artistic and academic abilities and Anokhin's findings about the almost limitless potential of our minds to form patterns and connections have confirmed the current trend in thought that everyone's brain is much better than it has been given credit for, and that most of the problems we experience with the use of our brains are not because of any fundamental inability but because we have so far not received enough information about ourselves and the way we work.

Your Upper and Lower Brain

Yet another area where we have recently discovered a vast untapped potential is the relationship between the upper and lower brains.

The upper brain, variously called the rational brain, the "conscious" brain, the new brain, the intellectual brain, and, medically, the cerebral cortex, is the corrugated "thinking cap" that lies like a thick crumpled blanket over the central lower brain. The upper brain appeared at a later evolutionary stage and took over an increasingly large percentage of the cranial cavity, reaching its currently most advanced stage in mankind and the dolphins and whales.

Your upper brain deals primarily with intellectual activities, and it is useful to note here that when we refer to the left and right brain, we are actually referring to the left and right *upper* brain.

Your lower brain, variously called the subconscious brain, the old brain, the reptilian brain, the instinctive brain, and the emotional brain, handles all the day-to-day activities of which your conscious brain does not have to be particularly aware, including temperature controls, blood pressure, chemical balances, certain data processing, the digestive process, etc. Your lower brain also appears to be in charge of your emotions.

Your lower brain is the evolutionarily more primitive brain, and in the "lower" animals is in both volume and influence by far the most dominant.

Until as recently as 1970, it was thought that the upper and lower brains functioned relatively independently, and that the upper brain had no control at all over the lower brain's "automatic" functions, especially those relating to the control of certain bodily processes.

Then in March 1970, an Indian yogi, Swami Rama, visited the Menninger Foundation in Topeka, Kansas, where researchers were doing some exploratory work in the field of one of mankind's fondest dreams: the control of the body with the mind. In a series of experiments, Swami Rama was wired for brain waves, respiration, skin potential, skin resistance, heart behavior, blood flow in the hands, and temperature. While he was thus "wired up" he caused two areas a couple of inches apart on his right hand to change temperature in *opposite* directions. The rate of the temperature change was about 4° Fahrenheit per minute, and he was able to maintain the change until there was a temperature difference of 10°.

Swami Rama also demonstrated that he could "stop his heart" from pumping blood around his body. It was assumed by the researchers, Alyce Green, Thelma Green, and Dale Walters, that his heart would actually stop beating. What happened instead was that his heart began to fire at about three hundred beats a minute, without blood either filling the chambers properly or the valves working properly.

In addition to these experiments, Swami Rama also demonstrated that he was, with his brain, able to control his brain's own brain waves!

From this and many other subsequent experiments, we now know that it is possible for the upper brain to program the lower brain, and in so doing to affect physical health, athletic performance, mental abilities, motivation, and willpower.

In fact, in many "primitive" societies such abilities were taken for granted, although they were probably not related to the upper and lower brain. The aboriginals of Australia, for example, had what may be considered a far more advanced form of justice than that of some of our more recent Western societies. If a member of the tribe had committed an act which both the tribe and the individual thought was punishable by death, they talked the matter over first and came to a unanimous agreement, upon which the convicted individual simply went away and within one day, using the power of his brain only, had one by one turned off all bodily processes until he had committed a self-induced execution.

At the opposite extreme, there are many instances of individuals "miraculously" recovering from illness, damage, and disabilities which were later attributed to their power of mind.

Similarly, many children, especially when examinations are approaching, can give themselves nosebleeds, change their body temperatures, change their blood pressures, and produce vomiting, spasms, and any number of skin rashes. In each instance it seems that once again the upper brain is controlling the lower in order to produce a desired result.

The same effects can be observed in champion athletes. In golf the best players regularly say that at their level of competition the game is 20 percent physical and 80 percent mental self-programming. In tennis the same applies; Billie Jean King was considered by her opponents to have no particular physical area in which she was superior to everyone else, but they unanimously agreed that once she had really programmed her body with her mind to win, there was no way of beating her unless they could program themselves even better.

One of the greatest examples of control over both his own and other brains was the boxer Muhammad Ali. He would program into both his own and his opponent's bodies "future memories" in which entire sequences of events, from the signing of the fight contract to the probable round of the knockout, would be repeatedly etched into both his own and his opponent's brain.

With this newly acquired knowledge and evidence, how can you apply this extraordinary knowledge to your own life?

Positive Positive Thinking

The technique for making your brain work well for you rather than against you is to apply advanced forms of positive thinking.

Negative thinking, or a negative "mental set," quite simply and obviously programs your brain to work against itself and you. There is also a danger, often experienced but seldom understood, that positive thinking can also produce a negative result. Consider the following example. A golfer, on the fifth tee of a certain course, shoots into a waterhole in three consecutive matches. Knowing about the functions of his upper and lower brain, he decides to take some positive action, and programs himself not to go into the same waterhole next time. He spends months programming himself this way, gets to the fifth tee for the fourth time, and to his amazement and discouragement goes straight into the waterhole again.

Why?

The reason lies in the subtlety of the brain, and the necessity for great care in self-programming. What the unfortunate golfer was unwittingly doing was programming both his brain and his body to concentrate almost entirely on the waterhole, rather than on his *real* goal, which was the far green. In other words, he was putting a positive onto a negative and constantly, although unaware, expanding the negative.

What is essential in positive thinking is to program a positive onto a positive. Thus, never program yourself not to get ill; program yourself to get better, visualizing yourself in full health. Never program yourself not to fail; program yourself to succeed, visualizing your goal. Never program yourself not to be stupid; program yourself to become increasingly bright and alert, again visualizing your goal.

One of the best ways to establish an ongoing and positive relationship between your upper and lower brains is to clarify your goals and objectives, and then to repeat your positive-on-positive instruction to yourself while visualizing as imagistically as you can your objective. If this can be done when you are in an especially relaxed state, so much the better, as relaxed and hypnagogic states allow the communication channels between the two brains to flow more freely.

If you are especially interested in developing this aspect of your mental power, it is well worth investigating the areas of autosuggestion, self-hypnosis, meditation, visualization, and self-programming. The results will please and often astound you, and can be done throughout your lifetime, building up an increasing motivation and willpower with practice.

Improving with Age

One final bit of good news about our brains has come from the research of Professor Mark Rosenzweig and others.

For far too long it has been assumed that the brain declines with age, reaching a peak between the ages of eighteen and twenty-four, and deteriorating steadily from then on. This decline was held to include most mental abilities—among them recall, retention, numerical ability, creativity, alertness, and vocabulary. These beliefs were supported by common sayings such as "You can't teach an old dog new tricks."

All of these mistaken beliefs can now be comfortably laid to rest. Professor Rosenzweig has shown that if the brain is stimulated, *no matter at what age*, it will physically grow more protuberances on each brain cell's tentacles, and that these protuberances will increase the total number of connections within the human brain.

Apart from these scientific findings, history is dotted with great minds who showed that ability was not dependent on age, among them Gauguin, who did not really start to paint until his thirty-fifth year; Michelangelo, who was producing great works of sculpture, art, and writing into his eightieth year; Haydn, who wrote some of his most

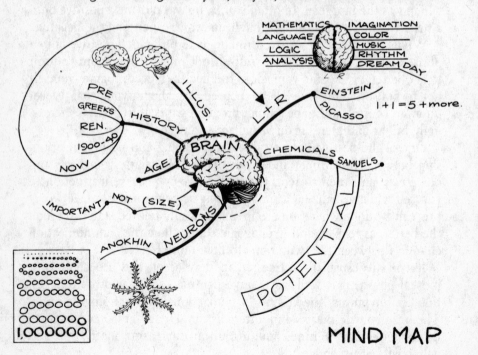

MIND MAP

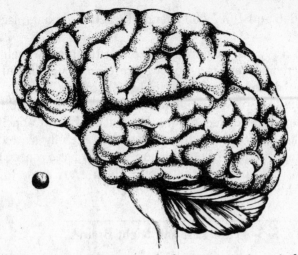

The complexity of the world's entire telephone systems is equivalent to a part of your brain the size of an ordinary garden pea.

beautiful music in the latter years of his life; and more recently again, Picasso, who was producing copiously into his nineties.

Evidence is also found in other societies, in which the elder members of the community were always considered to be the "Wise Men," a description which covered not only their knowledge and experience, but also their ability to use the knowledge they had.

In the light of all this, the old contention that we lose brain cells continually throughout our lives and that this causes serious mental decline fades into insignificance. Apart from the fact that we can generate new connections far more rapidly than the average loss of brain cells, it can also be shown that even if we lose 10,000 brain cells a day from the time we are born, we have started with so many that the total number lost by the age of eighty would be less than 3 percent.

Your Brain—Some Comparisons

The brain is often compared with machines and electrical systems, but what we now know about the brain makes this pretty hard on the machines. It has been calculated, for instance, that the entire network of the world's telephone systems, if properly compared to your brain, would occupy a part of it the size of an ordinary garden pea.

And it has been suggested that at any given moment there are between 100,000 and 1,000,000 chemical reactions taking place in your brain.

We have really just begun to realize that the human brain is a biological supercomputer, and that we are even now still only on the threshold of discovering its extraordinary abilities. Among our first priorities must be an exploration of the way it functions, and the development of exercises or techniques that will enable it to operate more naturally and effectively. This can be most usefully started by first looking at the workings of our memory and our basic senses, and then adapting our knowledge of the brain to help every sense to function more smoothly and easily.

SELF-CHECK 3—Your Left and Right Brain

How "balanced" is your weekly activity? On a separate sheet of paper make a note of the various activities in which you engage during a week, the amount of time you spend on each activity, and the percentage of left and right brain involved in the activity. When you have completed the list, make a check of your overall percentage, and think about whether you need more general balance in your life. Most people in the United States spend roughly 70 percent of their waking time involved in left-brain activity and only 30 percent involved in right-brain activity.

2

Your Memory Can Be Better Than You Think

How often do you say, "It's on the tip of my tongue," or "My head's like a sieve"? In this chapter evidence is given to show that your memory is better than you think. Special sections deal with self-checking, organizing your time to make sure that memory is maximized, reviewing techniques to make sure that forgetting is held to a minimum, and remembering lists. Outlines are given for solving the major memory problems: remembering names and faces, and remembering to link things together.

The final section explains how you can "set" yourself to remember, and gives examples and personal histories of the great memorizers.

KEY WORD SUMMARY

Checking your current position
Storing
Retrieving
Organizing time
Linking
Emphasizing
Reviewing
Link memory system
Names and faces
Setting yourself

SELF-CHECK 4—Checking Your Current Position

Before reading this chapter, try a simple check. It's like a game we played as children, trying to memorize the objects on a tray.

Below is a list of words (don't look at them yet!). When you have

finished reading these instructions, read through the list at your normal speed, one word at a time, *making sure you do not go back over
any words you have read*. There are too many words in the entire list
for you to remember them all, so the task is simply to remember as
much as you can.

pay
head
turn
now
fee
field
the
of
left
and
to
of
which
the
will
once
and
more
clearly
Mao Tse-tung
together
inch
and
the
then
of
they
actual
of
and
case
the
repeat
same
other

Now turn the page, without looking back, and answer the questions.

1. How many of the first six words in the list can you remember?

_____   _____   _____   _____   _____   _____

2. How many of the last six words can you remember?

_____   _____   _____   _____   _____   _____

3. Can you remember any word which appeared more than once?

4. Can you remember any word or group of words that was outstandingly different from all the others?

5. Can you remember any other words?

This little check on memory is designed to see not *how much* you remembered, but *how* you remembered. In the following pages a special section is devoted to improving any areas of weakness.

Memory Improves with Age

"Difficulties with memory" are commonly mentioned by people when asked what problems they have in using their brains.

In fact, this has become almost institutionalized, and society now generally accepts that most of us have poor memories, and that memory declines as we get older. Some people even go so far as to congratulate themselves on their declining memory, and it is not uncommon to hear half-apologetic, half-self-satisfied conversations like: "My memory is not nearly so good as it used to be." "Yes, I know exactly what you mean; mine's not so good anymore either."

Actually, the reverse is true. To confirm this, let us look at the different aspects of memory: how memory changes as time progresses *while* we learn and *after* we have learned, and how we can look after our memory in such a way as to make sure that it remembers what we want it to remember, and that it progressively *improves* with age.

Retention and Recall

Memory can be divided into two aspects: retention and recall. Retention is the ability of the mind to take in and store information. Recall is the ability to select from that vast store the special piece of information we need at any given time.

When people complain of having a "bad memory," they do not really mean that their entire memory is bad, but normally that their ability to *recall* something is temporarily weak.

This is perhaps best exemplified by the "tip of the tongue" feeling. In this situation the person *knows* that he knows something and will say, "It's on the tip of my tongue, but I can't *remember* it." What he really means is that his brain has retained the information, but that he cannot at that moment *recall* it.

If a case is to be made for the improvement of memory (and for most people this means the improvement of their recall) it is necessary first to establish that the store of information is there to be drawn from. Fortunately, there is considerable evidence to support the suggestion that our brains do retain far more information than is generally thought—perhaps, even *all* of it.

Retention—the Evidence

1. NEAR-DEATH EXPERIENCES. When people have been confronted with a truck bearing down on them or have fallen off a cliff or nearly drowned, and have somehow miraculously survived, they have reported that their entire life flashed before them just before they lost consciousness. On further questioning, they have insisted that it was not just a few important events, but their *entire* life. These experiences are reported by people of all ages and races, and are often given with considerable embarrassment, because the individual, not knowing that the experience is common, thinks something is wrong with him.

2. CONVERSATION. Because normal conversation is so commonplace and automatic, we tend not to notice the complex process taking place. When you listen to another person talking, automatically understanding as the conversation progresses, your brain is doing the most fantastic piece of retain/recall manipulation, checking in its storage banks for every word uttered, comparing it with all the previous times that that word has been uttered, and then making a long series of sense-links to guarantee that you experience a smooth and continuous flow of understanding. The speed and subtlety of this process is so extraordinary that you don't even notice it. By comparison, the most sophisticated computer in the world will be left far behind your brain within two seconds.

3. DREAMS. Many people experience dreams in which characters and situations appear after they had been "forgotten" for as many as fifty years—old school friends, first loves, and so on. The vision of these people and places in the dream is usually described as completely clear, and surprising in its accuracy of detail.

4. HYPNOSIS. Under competent supervision, people have been able to "unlock" memory banks, releasing entire sections of their lives which for some reason they had been unable to recollect. When these hypnotic releases take place, the recall is once again exceptionally clear, indicating that the storage process throughout has been extremely accurate.

5. SURPRISE STIMULUS. In these situations you suddenly see, hear, touch, taste, or smell something which "triggers off" an entire series of connected memories.

Many people experience this when returning to areas in which they once lived but have long since left. One of the most common is a return to an early school, where one whiff of aromas from the kitchen can bring back extremely pleasant or unpleasant memories.

6. EXPERIMENTS. The Canadian neurosurgeon Dr. Wilder Penfield probed the brains of his patients with tiny electrodes, looking for areas in the brain that were causing these patients to have epileptic fits. The patients remained conscious throughout the procedure, and to his surprise Dr. Penfield noted that sometimes when he excited the tiny electrode his patient would suddenly start "reliving" experiences from previous years, ranging from childhood to the day before the testing.

This happened time and time again with different patients, and upon checking with relations and people who had been present at the "relived" experiences, Penfield found that the brain was somehow being stimulated to total sensory recall of the event. He found that these events seemed to be stored over the surface of the brain, and suggested that if we could find the right clues it might be possible to unlock every event of a lifetime.

7. PHYSIOLOGICAL EVIDENCE. The work done by Professor Anokhin and Rosenzweig suggests that the brain does have the physical capacity to store most of the information that is fed into it. Rosenzweig calculated that even if the brain were fed ten new bits of information every second for its entire life, it would be nowhere near full.

8. SPECIAL MEMORY SYSTEMS.   Special memory systems have been used by stage magicians and professional memorizers for centuries. Experiments showed that by using these systems anyone could remember unconnected items in random, ordinary, and reverse order, with complete accuracy, even though they were given each new piece of information at the rate of one every two seconds. Performance dropped off only when people became bored.

9. FAMOUS MEMORIZERS.   The man most famous for having a "perfect memory" was a Russian called S. S's memory was so good that if you asked what happened on a given day fifteen years before, he would pause for a moment and then respond with the question: "At what time?"

S was studied for many years by the Russian psychologist Aleksandr Luria, who confirmed that somehow, at an early age, S's brain had "clicked" into natural methods for retaining and recalling everything in his life. In all other respects, including the structure and general functioning of his brain, S was apparently like any other human being.

Your Recall—and How It Works

Knowing that the storage capacity of the brain *is* so great, we can now turn our attention to the second aspect of memory: recall.

There are five main factors which assist your memory to recall:

1. primacy
2. recency
3. linking
4. outstandingness
5. review

1. PRIMACY.   All other things being equal, you will recall the beginning of events more than the middle of events, and will recall a first event more than continued repetitions of that event. Thus, in the little memory check at the beginning of this chapter, you will probably have recalled quite a few of the first six words: pay, head, turn, now, fee, field.

2. RECENCY.   Again, all other factors being equal, you will tend to recall events which are very recent. In the list you may have recalled one or two of the last four or five words: case, the, repeat, same, other.

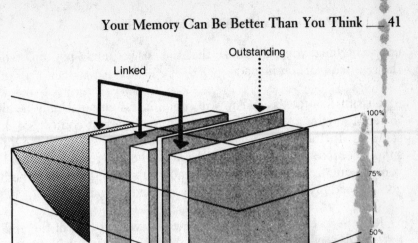

Recall during learning. As this graph shows, when you are learning something there are four main areas of highest recall: the beginning; the end; things which are linked; and things which are outstanding.

In real-life terms it shows that you will recall yesterday better than the day before that, the day before yesterday better than the day before it, and so on.

This tendency extends even into very old age, where people will be inclined to remember the events of early childhood and the events of recent days, but not so much of their middle years—even to the extent of confusing the generations of their own family.

3. LINKING. You will recall anything which is connected better than something which is disconnected. In the list you will therefore have remembered the repeated (linked to themselves) words: and, of, the.

If you pause for a moment to think about the way you normally recall something, you will realize that the answer does "pop up" when the right *connection* is made.

4. OUTSTANDINGNESS. You will more or less automatically be able to recall anything which is strange, unusual, out of context, or outstanding. In the list you will probably have recalled Mao Tse-tung, simply because it was so different from all the other words. In real life your experience will confirm that really outstanding events, whether good or bad, usually remain indelibly marked in your mind.

5. REVIEW. Many physiologists now believe that part of the ability to recall depends on the "strength of the brain pattern" laid down biologically and electrically. They emphasize that this strength is increased by repeating the memory pattern. In practical terms, this means that anything which is reviewed will tend to be more firmly lodged in the brain than something which is simply skimmed over once and left to recede.

Applying This Knowledge   The knowledge that the brain recalls first and last things best is useful in any learning situation, for it helps us to organize time in such a way as to increase recall. For example, if you study for four hours without a break, you will be giving yourself only one primacy and one recency situation, allowing your recall to sag in the middle. Breaking the four hours into more reasonable units will provide a greater number of "first and last" situations, and a consequent rise in recall. These time units have to be long enough to enable the mind to build up a rhythm, and short enough to prevent it from having too large a sag in the middle. Experience now indicates an ideal study time of between ten and forty-five minutes, depending on such things as the difficulty of the subject and your level of interest. Organizing learning periods in this way not only helps recall, but also leaves you far more rested at the end of the learning period, because in the breaks (which should normally be between two and five minutes) your mind has had a chance both to rest and to sort out the information it has been taking in during the learning period.

The fact that linking assists recall can be applied in a number of ways. It is obviously vital for comprehension and understanding, and can be used with great effectiveness in note-making and the organization of study. You can assist yourself in learning by consciously looking for the links between the units of information which are being given to

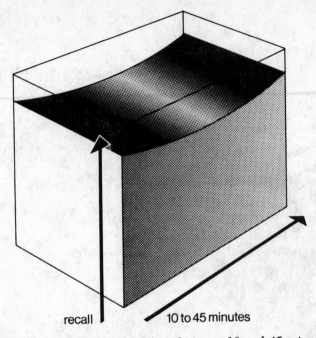

recall   10 to 45 minutes

Ideal study time. The ideal study time is between 10 and 45 minutes. This ensures that the beginning and end periods of recall are high, while also making sure that the middle period is not so long that it sags down.

you. (Chapters 6 and 7 on note-making and creativity will help you to develop this concept further.)

Knowing that your brain recalls things which are outstanding, you can assist your recall by mentally trying to emphasize those areas you particularly want to remember. This means making things larger than life, giving them extra-bright or contrasting colors, and placing them in situations that make them "stand out." (Specific examples and techniques are expanded in the section later in this chapter dealing with special memory systems.) Outstandingness can also be applied to note-making situations.

The Importance of Review

Proper reviewing or revision does not mean a blind repetition of information, but means an organized series of special times for looking at information already understood. Normally, after only four or five re-

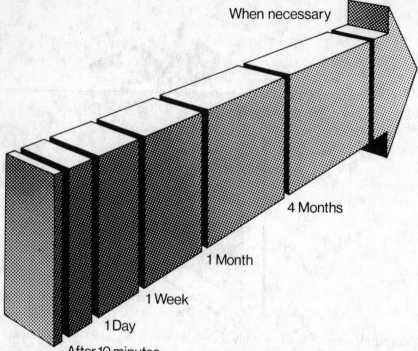

When necessary

4 Months

1 Month

1 Week

1 Day

After 10 minutes

Review. In order to make sure you do not forget, review needs to be done at the correct time and intervals. The diagram shows a sample review graph for a one-hour learning session. Each review should not take more than five minutes, and the later ones need take only one or two minutes.

views, the information being reviewed will enter the "long-term memory"—that part of your memory where information like your name, address, and normal vocabulary is stored for immediate and automatic recall.

Review should be sensibly spaced out. This normally means that after a period of learning, your mind should be given a short period for rest and integration—say, ten minutes—followed by a first review. The second, third, fourth, and fifth reviews can take place at increasing intervals, something like a day for the second, a week later for the third, a month later for the fourth, four months later for the fifth.

It is important to remember that reviewing is performed only on the information you really wish to remember, and not on *all* the information you might have taken in while reading the book or listening to a lecture. This ability to select the specific information needed for review can be usefully combined with the ability to extract key words and key areas of meaning. (Techniques for improving this ability are discussed in Chapter 6.)

The other advantage of proper reviewing is that the more the information your brain already contains is reviewed, the more easily you will be able to latch on to new, incoming information.

The brain which has forgotten most of what it has learned will find new learning far more difficult than the brain which is completely up to date and is ready to compare, contrast, and connect the incoming information with the information already stored.

The situation is reminiscent of the biblical saying: "Unto him that hath shall be given . . . but from him that hath not shall be taken away even that which he hath." By him that has much knowledge, new knowledge shall more easily be gained; by him that has little knowledge and does not review, new knowledge shall be difficult to acquire, and the little knowledge that he does have will tend to be forgotten.

Special Memory Systems

These memory systems, once described as tricks, are now known to be based on two of the major aspects of memory: linking and outstandingness.

The simple rules for these systems number only two.

1. LINKS. You must make dramatic and simple links between the things you want to remember, or between the things you want to remember and specially prepared memory code lists. This means that you bang things together, place things on top of each other or underneath each other, blend them with each other, or substitute one for the other.

2. OUTSTANDINGNESS. You must exaggerate in every way possible the combined image, using all your senses in the process. This means that the combined image must be much larger than life, garishly colored, humorous or absurd; and you must, where possible, be able to imagine yourself tasting, touching, hearing, seeing, and smelling it.

One of the simplest basic mnemonic techniques is that known as the link system, in which a series of items is simply remembered by applying the two basic rules.

For example, if a man has to phone another businessman about a contract as soon as he gets into the office; has also to phone his wife, and write letters confirming a lunch appointment, adjusting his accounts, and reserving an airplane ticket; has to meet a television producer in the afternoon; and has to buy a bottle of wine, peas, and paper napkins on the way home, he might remember all this in the following way:

Out of one end of the phone, like the genie out of the lamp, he could imagine his business partner emerging and waving the gigantic contract about which they have to talk on the phone. From the other end of the phone would emerge his wife, juggling with peas and wiping up a broken bottle of wine with paper napkins.

This entire scene he could then imagine as being presented to him on a gigantic television screen.

To remember the three letters—and allowing his imagination really to exaggerate in order to make best use of the mnemonic techniques—he might imagine an enormous lunch on top of the television set, with thousands of dollar bills fluttering onto it, dropped from an airplane flying overhead.

This example sounds ridiculous, absurd, and exaggerated. It is! And the effectiveness of the technique will become clear when you realize that even though this example has nothing to do with you, the reader, you'll have difficulty forgetting it.

A number of people are already using these systems in both home and professional life. Businessmen, for example, can use such a system to enable them to remember the person they have to call as soon as they get into the office, the significant letters they have to write, the major appointments for the afternoon, and the items they have to pick up from the store on their way home.

It can also be seen that these systems, once considered "tricks," are soundly based on the way our brains work. They utilize that enormous range of abilities that continually lies dormant in the right brain, waiting only for the opportunity to express itself.

Memory and Observation—Remembering Names and Faces

It is impossible to remember something your senses have not properly taken in. Memory is consequently largely dependent on the way in which you "allow things in," and this will be dealt with in detail in the following chapters on listening and seeing. Meanwhile, it is appropriate to see how observation can be used to overcome one of the most common of all memory problems: remembering names and faces.

Many people, when introduced to others, "know" that they are going to forget the names anyway and therefore go through a whole series of introductions without looking at one of the faces to whom they are being introduced. Their fear of failure actually guarantees that they do fail. Even those who do look at new faces will often tend to see the "general face" and not really look at its specific characteristics.

Because your recall works by linking and also by outstandingness, it is essential when seeing a new face to look at it properly, so that you can take any opportunity for linking or remembering outstanding features. This does not mean peering rudely at the person's face, but simply taking an active, intelligent interest.

You can prepare your mind for this by "exercising" your observational powers in public places. At different times give yourself different parts of the face to look at, so that on one day you might concentrate on noses, another day on eyebrows, another day on ears, another on general head shapes, etc. You will find to your surprise that each part of each face varies enormously from person to person, and that your increasing observation of the differences will assist you to remember the new faces that you meet.

In order to assist your recall even further you can use linking and review techniques when being introduced. If it is reasonable, ask for the name to be repeated, and then use it politely in the conversation that follows. It is far more considerate of the person you have just met to use his or her name than to refer to "you" or "he" or "she."

In order to establish links, it is often useful to inquire about the derivation of the person's name. This is not impolite, and most people have a fairly deep knowledge of, and interest in, the heritage of their names. During the conversation, if there is anything outstanding about either the face or the name, try to form imaginative links using the same techniques as outlined for the special memory systems.

The pleasant thing about this approach to remembering names and faces is that the more it becomes successful the more confident and open you will become, making the next memory task even more simple.

SELF-CHECK 5

Read this paragraph *without skipping ahead*. At the end of the paragraph you will find another paragraph, and your task is to read the second paragraph aloud, *once through only*, memorizing whatever you can as you read through, *without looking back*. When you have completed the paragraph, go on and answer the questions that follow. Start reading aloud the next paragraph *now:*

Five, sock; three, chicken; eight, chair; four, plant; two, red; ten, paper; seven, boat; one, sand; six, window; nine, body.

Now answer the questions.

Questions for Self-Check 5

Next to each number, write in the word that you read with that number in Self-Check 5.

1. _____
2. _____
3. _____
4. _____
5. _____
6. _____
7. _____
8. _____
9. _____
10. _____

The average score on this is between two and five, but with the use of the information you have been given in the book so far, combined with a special memory technique called the number shape technique, you can get ten out of ten every time.

The Number Shape Memory Technique

The number shape memory technique is one of those special memory systems initially developed by the Greeks, to allow you to tap the almost limitless potential of your memory.

This technique links numbers to objects which have the same shape as the number. To memorize a list you then simply link whatever you want to remember to the vibrant number image-shapes of your system.

The number shape memory system uses the numbers one to ten, and the key image words for each number are as follows:

1.	Pen
2.	Swan
3.	Breasts
4.	Sailboat
5.	Hook
6.	Golf club
7.	Cliff
8.	Hourglass
9.	Pipe
10.	Bat and ball.

For this memory system to work well, it is advisable for you to draw little sketches next to each number, so that you have the image-shape for the number clearly emblazoned in your mind. In the space provided, make quick sketches, next to the appropriate number, of the pen, the swan, the breasts, the sailboat, etc.

Number   *Number Image-shape*

1.

2.

3.

4.

5.

6.

7.

8.

9.

10.

Armed with the number shape memory system, the previous memory test becomes extraordinarily simple. All you have to do is use your right brain, your imagination, and your ability to make linkages and outstanding pictures, and you'll score perfectly.

For example, going back to your original memory check:

—to remember that number one is "sand," you imagine a *gigantic* pen writing messages on an enormous beach;

—to remember that number two is "red," you picture your swan covering the entire sky with brilliant and luminescent red feathers as it flies from one side of your vision to the other;

—to remember that number three is "chicken," you imagine a gigantic chicken with size 400 breasts;

—to remember that number four is "plant," you imagine a beautiful sailboat, similar to those sailed in the America's Cup race, which suddenly sprouts from every board in its deck plants which entangle the sails and the sailors;

—to remember that number five is "sock," you imagine your gigantic hook being used as a washing line on which there are nothing but socks;

—to remember that number six is "window," you imagine yourself swinging your golf club, and it's flying out of your hand and crashing into a gigantic plate-glass window;

—to remember that number seven is "boat," you imagine a gigantic ocean liner crashing into a rocky cliff;

—to remember that number eight is "chair," you imagine an enormous hourglass sitting on a chair, the sand spilling out onto the seat and dripping down over the legs;

—to remember that number nine is "body," you imagine yourself smoking a pipe out of which, like the genie from Aladdin's lamp, emerges a dancing body of your dreams;

—and to remember that number ten is "paper," you imagine your favorite bat-and-ball sportsman swinging frantically at a ball, but being blinded in the process by mounds of paper that fall out of the sky on to him or her.

Even though you were not being specifically tested in the preceding paragraphs, you will find that your memory has latched on to a number of the ideas anyway. So now go on to self-check 6.

SELF-CHECK 6

In the space below write down, next to the numbers, first the number image-word, and next to each number image-word the word used in the preceding example.

Numbers	Number image-word	Test word
1.	_____	_____
2.	_____	_____
3.	_____	_____
4.	_____	_____
5.	_____	_____
6.	_____	_____
7.	_____	_____
8.	_____	_____
9.	_____	_____
10.	_____	_____

Number right _____ out of 10. _____ out of 10.

Total number right _____ out of 20.

An untrained memorizer would score between 3 to 7 out of 20! Compare your own score against this, and you will probably find a great improvement.

The number-shape system and others like it can be used for memorizing shopping lists, odd thoughts which at the moment you can't write down, special facts, etc. These systems can also be used for entertainment and party games, and perhaps most important of all for training the right side of your brain regularly to make outstanding and creatively memorable pictures. In fact, these systems lie at the heart of memory, and their basic rules were those rules applied by the historically great memorizers of all time, as you will realize when you read the following brief histories and their own approaches to their memories.

The Great Memorizers

History has been dotted with great memorizers, and it is useful to study them not only for historical interest, but also to make use of the techniques they used and to reconfirm the fact that the human brain has a fundamentally limitless storage capacity. By reading about the great memorizers and practicing what they practiced, you can set your own brain on the same path.

Antonio de Marco Magliabechi   Antonio de Marco Magliabechi was born in Florence, Italy, on October 29, 1633, to parents who could afford no education for him. He was apprenticed to a local fruit dealer and spent his spare time poring over waste sheets from printed books, which were used at the time for wrapping the groceries.

A local bookseller became interested in the boy's attempts to read and took him to his bookshop, where he rapidly learned to identify every book on sight alone. When he eventually became literate, he combined his reading ability with a virtually photographic memory, enabling him to remember most of what he read in its entirety.

This was put to the test when he was given a manuscript (which he was able to read with remarkable speed) by an author who had heard of his abilities. Antonio returned the manuscript, and the author later pretended that he had lost it and asked the young man to recall what he could of it in order to help him. To his astonishment Antonio wrote out the entire book, missing not a single word or punctuation mark.

He read and memorized increasingly large volumes of books, and eventually became so renowned that he was consulted by experts in different fields for source material on their own subjects. When they came to him with questions, he would quote any of the authors he had ever read by book, word, and page. He was hired by the Grand Duke of Tuscany, who appointed him librarian. In order to take in even more material (the entire library!) Antonio developed his speed-reading abilities up to almost superhuman dimensions. It was reported that he could simply "dip" into pages, absorbing the gist of the entire page with one or two fixations, much to the wonderment of those who watched him.

Antonio combined a number of the elements discussed in this book. He not only had a remarkable memory and reading faculties, but also, by constant practice of these abilities, was able to maintain them until his death at the age of eighty-one. It is reported that until the very last he spent much of his later years in bed surrounded by books, which he would speed-read and memorize perfectly until he fell asleep!

Christian Friedrich Heinecken Christian became known as the "Infant of Lübeck," the town of his birth in Germany on February 6, 1721. At the age of ten months he could speak and repeat every word said to him; at the age of one year he knew and remembered every major event in the first five books of the Bible; by the age of two he had developed this to encompass virtually all the facts of biblical history; at the age of three he supplemented this further with a comprehensive knowledge of world history and geography, combined with learning to speak both Latin and French; and in his fourth year he had already begun to specialize, applying himself to the study of church history and religion.

At the age of four his studies were interrupted by illness, and he apparently calmly predicted his own death, which occurred shortly thereafter on June 27, 1725, when he was still under the age of four and a half!

George Parker Bidder George Parker Bidder was born in Devon, England, in 1806. He was initially known as a child prodigy in calculation, being able to give immediate replies to questions such as: "If a flea springs two feet, three inches every hop, how many must it take to go around the world, the circumference being 25,020 miles? Also, how long would it require for the journey if it took sixty hops every minute?"

"It would take 58,713,600 hops, requiring one year, three hundred and fourteen days, thirteen hours and twenty minutes."

As he developed his mental powers, Bidder applied himself to engineering, and eventually was elected to Parliament, where his mental powers made him not only even more famous but the dread of opponents. One actually appealed to the House of Lords that Mr. Bidder should not be allowed to remain in the room because nature had endowed him with qualities that did not place his opponents on a fair footing.

Bidder explained his techniques, and in his explanations can be seen the fact that his brain was using both calculating and mnemonic techniques throughout: "If I am asked the product of 89 times 73, the answer, 6,497, comes immediately into my mind. I multiply 80 by 70, 80 by 3, 9 by 70, and 9 by 3." It was just that simple. "But it works better if those figures, 5,600, 240, 630, 27, can be visualized as a column and held as a retentive image—like chalk on a blackboard—until the addition can be completed mentally." Apparently, George Bidder was gifted with a sort of *photographic* memory before photography itself was known. Bidder put it more fully when he stated: "In mental arithmetic, you begin at the left-hand extremity and you conclude at the unit, allowing only one fact to be impressed on the mind at a time. You modify that fact every instant as the process goes on; but still the object is to have one fact and one fact only, stored away at one time. . . . The last result in each operation, alone, is registered by the memory, all the previous results being consecutively obliterated until a total product is obtained."

Like Magliabechi, Bidder retained his abilities to the very end, being able to perform phenomenal memory and calculation feats until his death at the age of seventy-two.

Paul Charles Morphy Morphy was born in New Orleans in 1837, where he rapidly became a child chess prodigy. He rapidly developed into one of the greatest chess players of all time, yet was able to get by with very little close study of the game, as he was able to depend almost entirely upon his naturally developed ability to make images, and on his extraordinarily powerful memory. On his way to the world championship he acquired a degree in law, and learned four languages at the same time.

In addition to these astounding skills, Morphy became one of the first and perhaps the best experts in another field: blindfold chess. Morphy could not only play blindfold chess, which requires a totally perfect recall of every new position throughout the game, but was able to play *simultaneous* games blindfolded against opponents who were not.

Morphy also stated that he could remember every move in every game of the hundreds that he had played throughout his championship career, including those when he was blindfolded, the claim being backed up by the fact that nearly four hundred of his games have been preserved, because he was able to dictate them after the event.

It was also reported that in order to strengthen even his superpowerful memory, Morphy would regularly review games shortly after having played them.

The Russian S S, whom we have mentioned before, was a Russian journalist who in the early part of this century was hauled up in front of his seniors at an editorial meeting in Moscow for not taking notes of the editor's speech.

When they questioned him about his misbehavior, he became genuinely embarrassed, for he had never really understood the purpose of making notes. When he was pressed to prove that he did not need them, he repeated, word for word and inflexion for inflexion, everything the editor had said!

He was then introduced to the famous Russian psychologist Aleksandr Luria, who tested his memory over twenty-five years and claims that in virtually every detail it was perfect.

In his writings about his own memory, S confirmed that as a child he had acquired the basic memory techniques and that these had become a natural process with him, rapidly developing into perfect retention and recall.

In addition to his astounding memory, S also was capable of incredibly creative solutions to various problems, thus underlining the importance of right-brain imaging to both the memory and the creative processes.

Dario Donatelli Dario Donatelli is a modern young American recently graduated from the Carnegie-Mellon University in Pittsburgh, where he specialized in memory techniques.

Donatelli describes himself as quite normal, stating, "My memory is like anyone else's. There are probably hundreds of thousands of other people who, if they had the same interest in numbers and saw a reason to practice calculating and memory for a few years, would be faster than I am."

He displayed no special mnemonic abilities before he began his experiments at Carnegie-Mellon, but with practice he has become one of the top memorizers of all time, and has recently broken the world record for digital memory. The previous record was set in 1911 by a German mathematics professor who memorized eighteen digits without error.

Donatelli recently memorized the following number of seventy-three digits: 1518593765502157841665850611209488568677273114-1818610546297480129497496528.

Forty-eight seconds after being read the number he was able to respond: "The first set is 1518. Then 5937 . . ." He repeated all the digits in order, grouping them in groups of three or four.

When asked how he did it he replied, "The first set was a three-mile time, the second set was a ten-mile time, then a mile, then a half-mile, then a two-mile time, then an age, then a two-mile, then a mile, then a two-mile, then two ages, then an age, then the three-thousand-meter time, then a mile, then a date, then a mile, then a ten-thousand-meter time, then a two-mile time, then an age, then an age, then an age, and finally a two-mile time."

Donatelli had been using a memory system similar to the number shape system, but longer, in which he had produced pictures and images in order to break, four times over, a world record that had stood for nearly seventy years.

He is now approaching the magic 100, which he feels he will be able to accomplish in the near future.

If you are interested in appearing in *The Guinness Book of Records,* try using *your* extraordinary memory to beat him. As he says, there are thousands of people out there who should be able to do it.

"Setting" Yourself to Remember

In conjunction with the above it is important to be aware that your memory, if looked after, will continue to improve with age. The work by Rosenzweig, as outlined in the chapter on the brain, emphasized that stimulation increased the number of patterns in the brain. As these memory loops form what appears to be the bulk of the patterns, it is important to keep the mind stimulated, and to encourage retention and recall practices wherever possible.

Self-improvement Exercises

1. Start a program of learning new subjects and new languages, in order to increase the basic memory store.

2. Encourage in yourself any activity that you have noticed helps you to remember.

3. Pay attention to your dreams, checking carefully the memory images which you thought you had "previously forgotten."

4. Occasionally attempt to "take yourself back" to a period in your life, exploring *all* the elements of your life at that time.

5. Keep a diary using key words, special little drawings, and as many colors as possible.

6. Use the special memory systems and special memory system techniques for pleasure, for exercise, and for remembering.

7. Organize your learning time so that the primacy and recency effects are maximized, and so that the sag-in-the-middle during learning is minimized.

8. Review, making sure that your review takes place just before the memory of what you want to remember starts to drop.

9. Encourage the use of your right brain, as it is this side which provides you with the images and color that make remembering easier.

10. Try to see and sense things in as much detail as possible—the more detail you store, the easier will be your ability to recall.

If you do this, and continue to remind yourself to remember by regularly referring to your books on memory, by leaving reminder notes in appropriate places, by devising review schedules, and by asking other people to do "spot checks" with you, your mind and memory will provide you with increasingly better performance for the rest of your life.

3

Listening

Listening is a subject we hear far too little about—one that causes problems for too many people. But there are solutions to many of these problems, solutions which are outlined in this chapter. A special section explains the use of "key" listening, and is followed by a discussion of the relationship of listening to the other senses. As with memory, "setting" for listening is explained.

KEY WORD SUMMARY

Potential
Problems in concentration
Solutions
Selecting "keys"
Other senses
Setting

SELF-CHECK 7

A. Circle the term that best describes you as a listener.

Superior   Excellent   Above average   Average

Below average   Poor   Terrible

B. On a scale of 0–100 (100 = highest), how would you rate yourself as a listener?

_____

(0–100)

SELF-CHECK 8

How do you think the following people would rate you as a listener? (0–100)

> Your best friend _____
>
> Your boss _____
>
> Business colleagues _____
>
> Job subordinates _____
>
> Your spouse _____

SELF-CHECK 9

As a listener, how often do you find yourself engaging in these ten bad listening habits? First check the appropriate columns. Then tabulate your score using the key below.

LISTENING HABIT	FREQUENCY					SCORE
	Almost always	Usually	Some-times	Seldom	Almost never	
1. Calling the subject un-interesting						
2. Criticizing the speaker's delivery or mannerisms						
3. Getting overstimulated by something the speaker says						
4. Listening primarily for facts						
5. Trying to outline everything						
6. Faking attention to the speaker						

7. Allowing interfering distractions _____

8. Avoiding difficult material _____

9. Letting emotion-laden words arouse personal antagonism _____

10. Wasting the advantage of thought speed (day-dreaming) _____

TOTAL SCORE _____

Key: For every "Almost always" checked, give yourself a score of 2
      For every "Usually" checked, give yourself a score of 4
      For every "Sometimes" checked, give yourself a score of 6
      For every "Seldom" checked, give yourself a score of 8
      For every "Almost never" checked, give yourself a score of 10

Analysis of Self-Checks 7–9

SELF-CHECK 7. Of every hundred people who rate themselves, eighty-five give themselves a score of average or less. Fewer than 5 percent rate themselves as superior or excellent. On the 0–100 scale, the average rating is 55.

SELF-CHECK 8. Surprisingly, most people believe that their best friend would rate them higher than anyone else as a listener, including themselves!

Bosses were similarly assumed to rank people higher than they rated themselves, perhaps on the assumption that we do, in fact, either through fear or respect, tend to pay more attention to people in positions of authority.

Colleagues and subordinates tend to be rated at exactly the same as an individual rates himself—55 out of 100.

The most intriguing responses come to the spouse, husband or wife. In the initial stages of a marriage, spouses consider their partner would give them as high a score as their best friend. Unhappily, as time progresses spouses consider that their partner would give them a lower and lower score, eventually dropping well below the score they would give themselves.

SELF-CHECK 9. The average score in self-check 9 is 62, 7 points higher than what the average person tends to give himself. This suggests that when we break listening down into specific areas of competence, we rate ourselves better than we do when considering listening only as a generality.

Ideally, everyone would rate himself or herself as superior or excellent and would be so; the ratings of one's best friends, boss, business colleagues, job subordinates, and spouse would all be similarly very high, and the breakdown of individual listening habits would similarly give a very high total score. The reason why at the moment the scores tend to be low and enormously varying is that we learn very little about hearing as either a physical or mental process, and spend very little time in our formal education dealing with ways to improve it. The remainder of this chapter outlines your phenomenal hearing potential, deals with some of the main problems with listening and describes the ARCURRC breakdown of the listening process, subsequently giving you twenty keys to becoming an effective listener.

The Potential of Your Hearing Ability

Your ear is like the most remarkable musical instrument ever devised. It enables your brain to duplicate the sound of every other instrument, can replay entire symphonies, can select and reject sounds at will, and can communicate all of this perfectly to your brain.

Its capacity is astounding: it can discriminate between millions of different nuances in sound. Between the outer layer of the eardrum and your receiving brain there are tens of thousands of interdependent structures forming the complete unit.

Recent studies of the Mabaans, tribes living near the Sudanese border, have given us fascinating new information about our hearing. The Mabaans are noted for their gentleness of speech and the care they take never to shock their hearing apparatus. These studies showed that all the older members of the Mabaan tribe had hearing just as acute as that of the younger members of the tribe. In other words, there was no natural decline in hearing ability, just as Rosenzweig's studies showed that there was no general decline in mental ability with age.

Hearing, then, like our other abilities, seems to be far more sophisticated than we used to think, as well as being an ability which, if cared for, does not decline with age. Work by Dr. Gerd Jansen and others has also shown that listening plays a very large part in memory, that it is definitely linked to the other brain centers, and that it is one of the essential ingredients of imagination and creativity.

Why is it that our listening habits are so poor, and how can we both improve them and use them to the advantages of memory and our other senses?

Problems in Concentration

Among the main problems experienced in hearing and listening are the following:

1. physical
2. distractions
3. boredom
4. forgetting what was heard
5. indistinct sounds

1. PHYSICAL. Apart from those cases where physical damage is caused by disease, most of the decline in our hearing ability seems to

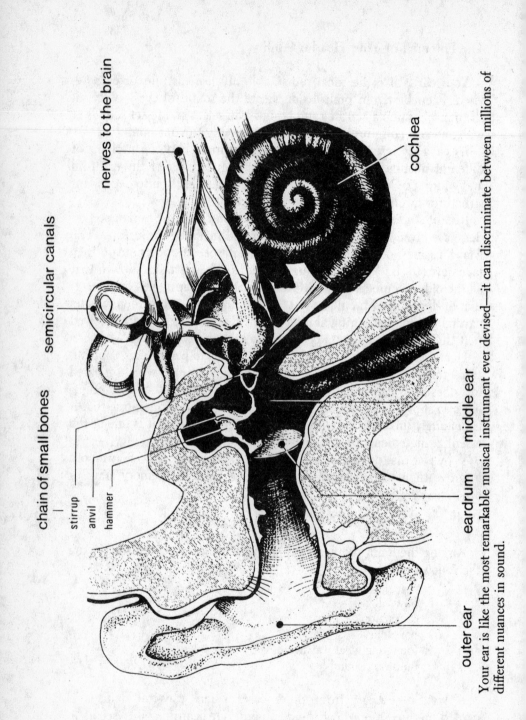

nerves to the brain

cochlea

semicircular canals

chain of small bones

stirrup
anvil
hammer

middle ear

eardrum

outer ear

Your ear is like the most remarkable musical instrument ever devised—it can discriminate between millions of different nuances in sound.

stem from the way we treat our hearing apparatus. It should be treated as a sophisticated musical instrument, which means keeping it in well-tuned running order and not abusing it.

In our society we continually bombard our very delicate inner ear with noises that are well above its tolerance level. Where possible it is advisable to avoid close contact with any large machine-generated sounds, especially airplanes and amplifying equipment. As the studies with the Mabaans emphasized, if the ear is looked after no decline need be experienced with age.

2. DISTRACTIONS.   Distractions to listening usually come from two main sources, the environment and our own internal thoughts.

One of the mind's astounding abilities is being able to reject sounds around us in which we are not interested. Thus, at a party, lovers can hear each other's whispered words despite the general havoc around. Similarly, a mother can detect the cry of her child above the shouting of a large crowd.

Simply being aware of this ability will often enable you to eliminate environmental distractions. Rather than concentrating on the noise which is distracting, concentrate on the thing you wish to hear, and the brain will automatically "switch off" the noises you wish not to hear.

Next time you are in a crowded gathering, be conscious of the things that you do hear, and the things that you do not listen to. You will find you are able to pay attention, despite the surrounding noise, to the person in whom you are interested, or to a conversation which contains information that is of importance to you. Notice how your mind and body "set themselves" to listen, and practice using this ability next time you are in a situation where the surrounding noise seems insurmountable. You will often find that it is not insurmountable at all—as shown by the many people who when shouted at or called by name have reported afterward that they were so intent on what someone else was saying they simply did not hear.

In the same way that it can switch off, your brain can also "switch on" its listening abilities. Many people can sleep through the most extraordinary nighttime noises, to awaken immediately at the whisper of a loved one or at the sound of a gentle alarm. Once again, knowing this capacity, it is advisable to practice and encourage it—the more it is used, the more it will benefit you.

This you can do by making a conscious decision to listen to any given set of sounds around. If you are on a busy street, decide first to listen to the sound of feet on the pavement, then to the sound of voices, then to the sound of car horns, then to the sound of birds, then to the sound of specific types of traffic. Similarly, when you are in your house, listen separately for the different sounds it makes: water sounds, wind sounds, electric sounds, movement sounds.

The second form of distraction results from our own personal thought processes. This can often occur when we are tired, or suffering from undue pressure. One of the most effective ways of eliminating such distractions is to organize the listening/learning situation so that understanding and recall are maximized (see the section "Your Recall—and How It Works" in the previous chapter). If this is done, your mind will tend to concentrate on the listening, and not "wander off" because of sagging recall and attention.

All this is very closely associated with another major listening problem:

3. BOREDOM. Boredom usually occurs in a situation where we are "obliged" to pay attention, but in which our interest has not been engaged. The result is usually a fairly immediate wandering of the mind, and an almost total loss of what is being said.

Apart from either leaving or endeavoring to pretend an interest we do not feel, one technique for highly boring situations is strongly recommended: that of the strongly opposed critic.

If you are listening to talk in which you are deeply interested, you will lean forward, "all ears." And this holds good when the speaker is opposed to your own beliefs, or is someone whom you particularly wish to argue against.

So lean forward, "all ears," when listening to something boring! Listen with your attention directed to a complete, constructive criticism of all that you are hearing. If you do this, your mind will readily take in all the information you are hearing.

4. FORGETTING. Forgetting what you have been listening to (or should have been listening to) can be embarrassing for you, and signifies a waste of your time as well as of the speaker's. Apart from looking after your hearing apparatus, conquering distractions from the environment and your own mind, and using the strongly-opposed critic's technique to battle against boredom, there are three more techniques you can use to improve your listening ability: self-motivation, setting yourself to listen, and key selection.

Self-motivation is very closely related to willpower and goal-directedness, both of which are among the most tried and tested methods of improving any mental performance.

Setting yourself to listen can be practiced by creating your own listening exercises, in which you actively set out to hear more of what goes on around you—at work, while traveling, in conversations, at parties, in the countryside, and while drifting off to sleep. Give yourself little personal tests for detecting the differences between tones of voice, the songs of different birds, and the general noise level at your work and home at different times of the day.

Key selection is based on the fact that your mind does not remember in lists, lines, and sentences, but by connecting key words and images to each other (see Chapter 6 on note-making and fast writing). To remember what has been said, concentrate not on the general flow of sentences, but on those key elements that are the basis of what is being said. As these key elements gradually build up, try to build a linked pattern of these elements in your mind, visualizing the overall map of ideas as the talk continues. Key selection will not only enable you to recall far more of what you have heard, but will also significantly increase your ability to understand what you are hearing, make appropriate comments, and ask intelligent questions.

5. INDISTINCT SOUNDS.   This listening problem, of a different order from the others, is most dramatically experienced when trying to follow what another human being is saying. People often miss the main elements of a conversation, lecture, or speech simply because they are reluctant to point out to the speaker that he is *mumbling*. As the speaker's intention is usually to get his information across, he will more often than not be thankful for a gentle reminder that he cannot be heard properly.

The ARCURRC Model

It will now be increasingly clear to you that hearing is not a single event, but a continuing process that can be broken down into a number of steps.

The ARCURRC Model outlines these steps, thus enabling you to get a clear picture of the entire process and to focus your attention on any area of the process that needs specific improvement.

The ARCURRC Model is composed of the following seven steps:

1.   assimilation
2.   recognition
3.   comprehension
4.   understanding
5.   retention
6.   recall
7.   communication/use

1. Assimilation   Assimilation refers to the physical ability of your ear/brain to absorb the sounds around you. If you have any doubt about your ability in this area, it is advisable to have an overall hearing checkup as soon as possible. Even if you feel that your assimilation is perfectly adequate, it may still prove interesting to go to a hearing specialist and have a general "hearing profile" done. As well as giving you additional self-knowledge, such a profile may help to define areas which you can either bring back to normal or develop beyond normal.

2. Recognition   Recognition refers to the ability of your brain to decode the data which have entered through your ear. It refers to the base level at which you will be able to recognize, for example, that a sound entering your brain was a word, a bird song, an engine running, etc. This part of the hearing process is developed very rapidly in the early stages of life, but can become stagnant during the later years, when many of us tend to "tune out." It is worth maintaining this skill by practicing listening for different nuances in sound in the same way as you can develop your seeing skills by practicing analytical looking (discussed in Chapter 4).

3. Comprehension   Comprehension refers to the ability of your brain to interpret accurately the data that enters it. Thus your ability, for example, to comprehend the meaning of a sentence spoken to you.

4. Understanding   Understanding refers to your brain's ability, after having assimilated and comprehended the information, to link that information to your already existing data store of knowledge. A good listener alertly and constantly develops this skill.

5. Retention   Retention refers to the ability of your brain to store the information it has heard. This can be aided by developing understanding skills, especially structuring and restructuring ideas as they are being presented to you. By referring to the mind map at the end of chapter 1, you will find examples of the above techniques and will see how effective they are for assisting your recall.

6. *Recall* Recall refers to your brain's ability to get back out of storage what has been retained. As with retention, this skill can be developed by structuring ideas as they are presented, as well as by the time management and special memory techniques outlined in the previous chapter.

7. *Communication/Use* This is the final stage of your listening, when the entire process goes full circle, and you use the information you have heard to communicate to others. This can take place at least four ways:

1.   spoken
2.   written
3.   representational
4.   communication with self (thinking)

When you have become a good listener and developed the various skills connected with the process, you will gain enormous insight into presentation skills, for you will structure your communication in such a way as to enable other people to listen to it most effectively, thus creating an interpersonal positive spiral in which all the participants assimilate, understand, and communicate increasingly well.

In order to develop the ARCURRC Model and your listening process more completely, apply the following twenty keys to effective listening.

The Twenty Keys to Effective Listening

1. *Maintain Aural Health* Make sure that your hearing apparatus is in good health. There are many specialists who can assist you in this area.

2. *Train Your Ears* Consciously practice "analytical hearing." This consists of getting yourself back to the "state of nature" in which your

mind and ears were attuned to *all* sounds in the environment, while at the same time concentrating on those that were most important. Follow the advice outlined in the previous paragraphs on self-motivation and setting yourself to listen.

3. *Maintain General Physical Health*   Mens sana in corpore sano— Latin for "a healthy mind in a healthy body"—is a sound observation. If you maintain a general physical fitness, especially aerobic, *all* your senses will improve, including your hearing.

4. *Listen Opportunistically*   When you are obliged to listen to something, even when it may be boring, always ask, "What's in it for me?" Don't just automatically discard it. It is often in those areas where we least expect value that value arises.

5. *Listen Longer*   It is often said that the wiser the person the less that person speaks and the more he or she listens. In any listening situation, try to withhold judgment until the speaker has finished speaking and your comprehension is complete. Try to avoid making a judgment before you have the whole picture.

6. *Listen Optimistically*   If you listen with the hope, belief, and mental set that you will gain value from the experience, you enormously increase the probability that your mind will find valuable relationships. In addition, the whole process of listening will become increasingly more enjoyable.

7. *Challenge Your Brain*   You can stimulate your brain and improve your overall learning and listening skills by occasionally exposing yourself to more "advanced" material. Try not to feel oppressed or to resist such difficult material, but to enter it with enthusiasm.

8. *Consciously Work at Listening*   Actively decide that listening is going to become one of your personal skills, and in listening situations exhibit a truly active mental and body state, rather than faking attention.

9. *Use Synesthesia*   Synesthesia is your mental ability to blend your various senses. When you are listening, keep your other senses, especially sight, actively involved. The more you can link your senses, the

better your hearing, attention, understanding and general learning will be. S, the Russian mnemonist, reported that in *every* listening situation, all his senses were working in harmony.

10. *Maintain an Open Mind* When words are spoken that press your emotional triggers, try to interpret them in a more objective light, and to understand the perspective from which the speaker speaks. Even if you disagree, realize that the points of view you are hearing are indeed points of view, just as are yours.

11. *Use Brainspeed* Your brain can think four to ten times faster than the speed of speech. Therefore, while you are listening, use your extra mental abilities to anticipate, organize, summarize, weigh, and compare arguments, listen between the lines, and interpret body language, etc. With especially slow speakers you can develop this skill more completely, rather than giving in to a tendency to daydream and lose concentration.

12. *Judge Content, Not Delivery* While listening, try not to get involved in a "superiority complex" concerning any inadequacies in delivery and style that the speaker might have. Concentrate fully on the content.

13. *Listen for Ideas* Your brain works more efficiently if it can grasp "wholes." Therefore listen for central themes rather than for individual facts. If you do this the facts will take care of themselves, linking easily to the main structures that your brain will construct when it listens for ideas.

14. *Take Mind Map Notes* In conjunction with listening for ideas, your comprehension, understanding, retention, and recall will be far greater if you take highly efficient Mind Map notes rather than standard lineal or list notes. Mind Map notes involve your entire left and right brains, and consequently improve overall listening performance dramatically.

15. *Disregard Distractions* If there are distractions, don't get hung up on them. Accept that they are there, and consciously remind yourself that your mind has the ability to block out, if it wishes, virtually anything it does not wish to pay attention to. Concentrate on the positive.

16. Take Breaks Wherever possible, make sure that you have breaks from listening every thirty to sixty minutes. These breaks will give your brain the time it needs for integration, as well as giving you far more of the primacy and recency effects as outlined in Chapter 2.

17. Use Your Imagination Although listening may seem to be dealing with left-brain words only, it is in fact a whole-brain process. So when you are listening to words, create, as much and as appropriately as you can, mental images of the ideas you are receiving.

18. Listen with Active Poise Develop the same physical attitude of poise and alertness when you are listening as an animal has when it is listening. Slouched and slumped postural attitudes will automatically collapse your listening abilities.

19. Remember You Can Continually Improve with Age All listening skills will improve if they are nurtured in a mental environment of positive thought about age.

20. Practice Speaking Communication Skills If you practice your own speaking communication skills, you will get a perspective on listening "from the other side." This will have the additional benefit of developing you in a more all-round fashion, and will beneficially complete the ARCURRC Model.

Addendum We spend between 50 and 80 percent of our waking hours communicating. At least 45 percent of that communication time is spent in listening. In schools the percentage is even higher, with students spending between 60 and 70 percent of their classroom time listening. And in the business world, listening is often cited as one of the top three most critically necessary managerial skills.

Despite this, listening is the skill taught least, as shown in this table:

	Listening	Speaking	Reading	Writing
Learned	1st	2nd	3rd	4th
Used	Most (45%)	Next most (30%)	Next least (16%)	Least (9%)
Taught	Least	Next least	Next most	Most

Hearing and Your Other Senses

Research is showing how closely our senses are linked with each other. The previous assumption that the loss of one sense sharpened another is now being questioned. It seems rather that the loss of one sense *forces* us to develop the remaining senses to their maximum, but that the more senses we have, the greater the potential ability of each.

This ability of the senses to support each other is perhaps most dramatically shown by the great memorizers like the Russian S. S continually emphasized in his conversations with the psychologist Aleksandr Luria that whenever he perceived something with any one of his senses, all the other senses automatically joined in and he received a complete sense impression. It was this that enabled him to remember so completely.

Hearing is an especially important sense, and like smell it is one that we have particularly neglected and abused.

Once you make the start in looking after it, you will experience a continuing spiral of progress. No longer will things go in one ear and out the other—they will remain in your brain.

Using and Caring for Your Eyes

When you consider the quality of vision of the great artist or the amazing coordination of hand and eye of the champion tennis player, you begin to glimpse the enormous inherent capacity of your eyes. Here we examine their potential and such interesting questions as where you see, how you see, and whether you see in the same way as other people. Games and exercises are described which will enable you to discover how your eyes function when they look at moving things, and when they look at still things. The relationship between your vision and your emotions, health, senses, and memory is explained and advice is given on ways in which you can develop your analytical observation, expand your visual ability, and use your imagination in order to see more clearly. The final section of the chapter gives exercises for eye care.

KEY WORD SUMMARY

Amazing facts
Where and how?
Eye movement; your movement
Emotions, health, senses and memory
Analytical observation; peripheral vision
Caring for your eyes

Amazing Facts About Your Eyes

Your eyes are another miracle of biological engineering. At the back of each there is an area the size of a thumbnail which contains 150,-000,000 separate light receivers. These light receivers can process millions of millions of photons (light-energy particles) per second.

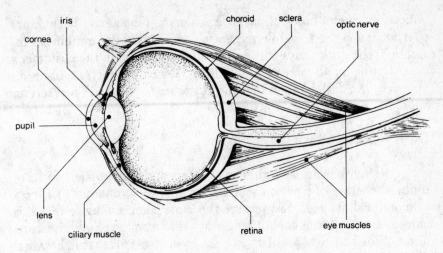

Your eye, like your ear, is a miracle of biological engineering. Each of your eyes contains 150 *million* separate light receivers.

As with our brain and the other senses, much general knowledge has now been gathered concerning our eyes, most of it helpful in enabling us to understand and improve the seeing process.

Seeing at the Back of Your Head

Paradoxically, we see at the back of our heads. A large area at the back of our brain called the occipital lobe processes all the information our eyes send to it via the optic nerve. This is one reason why it is particularly dangerous to hit someone on the back of the head, such a blow having been known to cause instant and permanent blindness.

Pupil Size

We have known for some time that pupil size adjusts according to light intensity and nearness. The brighter the light and the nearer the object, the smaller will the pupil size be.

Western scientists have recently discovered that pupil size also varies with emotion, and that if you are confronted with a sight that especially interests you (like a member of the opposite sex) your pupil size will automatically increase. Such changes are small, but can be noticed by careful observation. Jade dealers in China have been aware of it for many years. While presenting objects for the customer's inspection, the dealer pays particularly close attention to the customer's eyes, waiting for an increase in pupil size. When this increase has been observed, the dealer knows that the customer is "hooked" and sets an appropriate price.

Do You See as Others See?

A question which has intrigued thinkers and philosophers for centuries is whether one person sees the same thing as another. If I see a color and call it "red" and you see the same color and agree that it is indeed "red," we still cannot be certain that we are seeing "the same thing." For both you and I have been trained to call that light vibration, whenever we see it, "red"; but we do not know whether the same light vibration gives each of us an identical *internal* image.

In different moods the same things will be experienced as quite different. Witness the lovers who see everything through "rose-tinted spectacles," and the depressed person who sees everything as "black."

SELF-CHECK 10—Your Eye Movements

Before reading on, perform this little exercise: Look straight ahead of you, and imagine that an ordinary paperback book is being held up for you to read about one foot from your eyes. With your forefinger trace the speed and movement at which your eyes normally read. Do this now.

Most people move their finger in a smooth regular line, swinging from the end of one line to the beginning of another, much like the motion of a typewriter.

This idea of a smooth flowing motion is wrong, because our eyes can normally focus clearly on something only if they are still in relation to that object. If the object is still, the eyes must be almost still. If the object is moving, the eyes must move with it.

SELF-CHECK 11

To demonstrate this to yourself, try the following exercise. First hold the tip of your forefinger still in front of you, and focus on it intently, noticing what your eyes are doing. Next move the tip of the forefinger around, up and down and in zigzags, going to the very edge of your vision, all the while watching the tip *intently* with both your eyes.

You will have noticed that when your finger was still your eyes remained perfectly still, and that when your fingertip moved, your eyes moved with it, tracking it continuously.

SELF-CHECK 12

Now try another exercise. Put both hands up to the side of your head as if you are the victim of a holdup. Smoothly and simultaneously, move them across your face so that your arms make an X in front of you, then smoothly move them back to the original hold-up position. Throughout the exercise, visually follow each hand *individually*. As you perform the exercise, again notice your eyes' behavior throughout.

In that exercise you will have noticed that it was impossible to follow both hands at the same time, unless you are one of those rare people who can swivel their eyes independently.

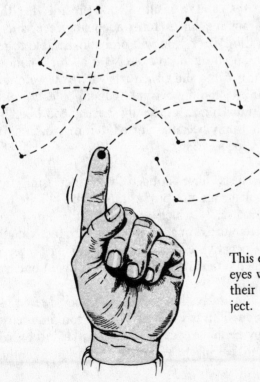

This exercise shows you how your eyes work when they are focusing their attention on a moving object.

These exercises serve to emphasize that our eyes need to "fix" on something if they are to see it clearly, in much the same way as a camera needs to be "held" on the object of the picture. For example, in order to take a picture of a moving car, the camera must move *with* the car. The resulting image of the car will be very clear, but will have a background that is completely blurred. This knowledge becomes especially significant in fast reading, as the next chapter will show.

It is also useful in various day-to-day situations. For example, many people in trains have great difficulty seeing the names on stations they are passing through, not because their eyes are unable to see, but because they don't use them properly. If they aimed their eyes on the name as it first appeared, and "fixed" on it as it went past, they would have a complete second in which their eyes held it still for them to read. This is better than vaguely looking out of the window and getting an impression of blurs as the train speeds through.

Relationship of Vision to Health, Emotions, Other Senses, and Memory

1. HEALTH. More often than not, a healthy body provides healthy vision. This, of course, means regular exercise, adequate sleep, and a well-balanced diet. If you think back, you will probably be able to recall that when for any reason you had no exercise at all for a period, both your body and vision became sluggish; that when you were not getting enough sleep, your eyes rapidly became red and "bleary"; and that when your diet was unbalanced, especially if laced too liberally with alcohol, your vision not only became blurred, but may even have disappeared momentarily altogether!

2. EMOTIONS. Eye specialists have noticed with increasing frequency that many eye problems are not physical in origin, but are the result of boredom or tension. Eyes which are continually bored "go slack" and will either receive blurred images or tend not to focus at all.

Similarly, tension has a negative effect on vision, forcing the eyes into a more rigid and strained observation pattern, resulting in unclear vision.

People in a state of dynamic relaxation or special alertness often report exceptionally clear vision. This is supported by the common-sense observation that very happy people's eyes seem to "sparkle," the simple reflection of good visual health.

3. THE OTHER SENSES.   Vision, like hearing, is intricately linked with all the other senses. The more extensively it is used, the "sharper" the other senses become. This close working harmony of the senses can be easily recognized if you remember the disturbance caused to your perception whenever sound and vision become unsynchronized on film or television.

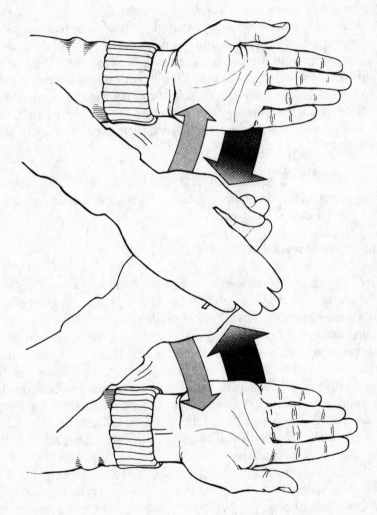

Hold both hands to the side of your head, and then move them evenly and smoothly back and forward in front of your face, looking at *each* hand clearly as they pass back and forward. This exercise will show you basic facts about how your eyes see.

4. MEMORY.   Vision is one of our most powerful sources of memory. The importance of correct observation becomes clear when we realize that our memory store is based on the information fed into it. If the eyes are letting through blurred images, the memory will not be able to operate as clearly or as accurately as it should. The relationship is almost direct: the more clearly and accurately we observe, the more clearly and more accurately will we remember.

Once again the perfect-memory man, the Russian S, made some relevant comments. He explained that when he was remembering something, he would often close his eyes and "re-see" the thing he had originally been observing. His original observation was therefore essential to his perfect memory. This habit of closing the eyes to remember something is not uncommon, and you often see people, when racking their brains for a visual memory, closing their eyes in order to see it more clearly.

In view of all this new information, it is now possible to recommend a series of exercises for expanding your observational abilities, and for taking special care of your eyes.

Exercises in Observation

1. ANALYTICAL.   When a baby is first born, all he can see is a great blur of confused shades of light. During his first few weeks, the brain sets about decoding the environment—"figuring out" what the various relationships are. This the brain does by storing the important pieces of information, and then continually checking them until the relationship of the object with its environment is clearly established. In this way the child rapidly learns to distinguish the difference between furniture and living beings, as well as the different functions for things, such as containing, pouring, and cutting. Once the basic distinctions have been made, the brain will often tend to take a rest, satisfied that all its labels are appropriate.

If the brain is left in this state, it will tend to become rigid and inflexible, learning little as the years progress, and developing bad recall habits, as exemplified by people who cannot remember names and faces, simply because they have labeled them all as "faces" without observing the distinctions.

The next and natural stage following the labeling is to look more closely at the makeup of the object labeled. This rapidly heightens gen-

Knowing how your eyes work can enable you to see things most people do not see.

eral awareness, as well as indicating that among the "same" objects there are an almost infinite number of variations. In order to develop this natural ability, it is necessary to exercise analytical observation. In fact, most readers will have exercised it in areas of their speciality, the artist having developed a special "eye" for art, the naturalist an ability to pick out different animals, birds, and plants at a glance, and a surveyor an ability to determine various structural aspects of buildings. What is essential is that this ability should be developed in all aspects.

The exercise is as follows:

"Set" your mind, at different times and on different days, microscopically to observe different aspects of your surroundings. The kinds of things you can concentrate on are horizons, the color of clothes, the differing shapes of plants, the posture and movement of people, the varying shades and shapes of clouds in the sky, and so on. In each of these exercises it is important to shift your focus continually, registering as many different parts of the complete object as you can.

A useful addition to this exercise is to practice analytical observation, and then to close your eyes and try to see completely in your mind's eye the object you have just observed. Next, open your eyes, check the real thing with your mental image, and close your eyes again, making any necessary corrections. Repeat this until the observed image and the mental image are identical.

This second part of the exercise not only increases your observa-

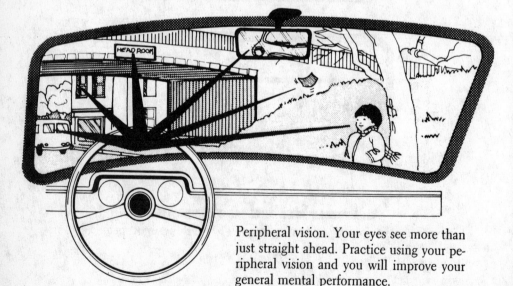

Peripheral vision. Your eyes see more than just straight ahead. Practice using your peripheral vision and you will improve your general mental performance.

tional abilities, but immensely improves both memory and creativity, by giving your brain a much larger and clearer store of images to draw from and to use in the making of new creative images.

2. PERIPHERAL. Supplementing your normal sharp-focus vision is an enormous and relatively unexplored area of vision known as peripheral vision. Of the 150,000,000 light receivers in the retina, only a small proportion lie in the region that is used for acute vision. The remainder are devoted to your peripheral vision.

This is the vision which prevents you from knocking things over, and which guides you during many of your movements. It is often called "unconscious" vision. "Superconscious" would be a more appropriate term, for its accuracy and efficiency are truly remarkable.

Peripheral vision also helps you to be "on the lookout" for things. If you have just bought a different model car, when you go for your first drive you will notice on the road other cars of the same model—regardless of whether they are directly in front of you or partially concealed in side roads. Similarly, anyone with a temporary or permanent obsession will continually pick out those items in the environment which relate to him.

This ability does not much depend on ordinary focusing, for often the things picked out are at the edge of the field of vision.

To increase this ability, practice "looking out of the sides of your eyes" while keeping them focused straight ahead. When you are sitting still, whether it be in your office or in a room at home, look straight ahead, focusing clearly on an object in front of you. Maintaining this fixed focus, look around the room, not in the way you normally do but with your "inner eye," seeing how clearly you can distinguish things far to the left, far to the right, above you and below you.

When you are a passenger (not the driver!) in a moving vehicle, similarly look straight ahead, paying special attention to all that is passing by at the *very edges* of your field of vision. This will include hedges, trees, houses, and other cars.

Peripheral vision is especially strong at night, because the numerous light receivers devoted to peripheral vision are sensitive to lower amounts of light than the sharp-focus receivers. Therefore, if you wish to see more clearly in the dark, don't look straight at the object you wish to see, for you will be focusing the wrong part of your eye on it. Practice looking at it from an angle of approximately 30 degrees and you will see it far more clearly.

The next chapter explains how techniques of observation can be applied to reading and to learning.

Keys for Caring for Your Eyes

You may find the following brief exercises useful for general eye care:

1. BLINKING. Most people "go tense" when paying special attention, or when reading. As a result they tend to stare, neglecting to blink. This causes eyestrain and prevents the necessary lubrication and circulation of blood to the eyes. Therefore, when you are concentrating on something, make sure that you continue to blink while you concentrate, as well as occasionally looking away and simply blinking while you rest your eyes.

2. PALMING. Whenever your eyes are doing a reasonable amount of work, give them regular small rests by closing your eyes and cupping them in your hands. This is best done by placing the base of the hand on the forehead. The hand should not touch the eye but simply form a little dome over it. During this rest period it is useful to imagine pure black, as this also gives the mind a rest from visual processing.

3. BREATHING. As with blinking, breathing tends to be "held" whenever we concentrate. This automatically causes tensions in other parts of the body, and vision is one of the areas that suffers. Therefore, whenever you are involved in long periods of concentration, try to make sure that your breathing is relaxed and regular. The benefits to your sight will be enormous.

4. FOR PEOPLE WITH GLASSES. The exercises in this and the next chapter apply to all people, whether or not they have glasses. Some have found that after doing the recommended exercises, they have been able to change to glasses one strength less than those they were wearing, because the relaxation of eye tension enables the eye to start to regain a positive process back toward its more natural state. Further gains can be made by ensuring that your glasses are always clean; by becoming conscious of the fact that it is often possible to improve

faulty eyesight; by visiting a specialist who emphasizes your eyes rather than your glasses; and by reading Aldous Huxley's *The Art of Seeing.*

5. LIGHT.   Daylight is always the best light for observation. Of the artificial lights, fluorescent is the worst, for it throws virtually no shadows. This tends to eliminate contrast, which is a vital part of seeing.

Each of these caring techniques, like the exercises, will assist both general vision and reading in particular—see the next chapter.

5

Speed Reading and Effective Reading

Why is the history of speed reading so controversial, and what are the reasons for the failure of certain speed-reading schools? This chapter answers these questions. The way your eye works and moves while reading is then explained and diagrammed, and special exercises help you to find out how your own eyes function as they read. New techniques are described for high-speed reading with the use of a guide. A special section outlines a complete method for handling reference, technical, and study reading. Finally, additional hints are given for "topping up" your reading speed and efficiency.

KEY WORD SUMMARY

History
Eye movement
Visual guiding
Study reading
Useful hints

SELF-CHECK 13—Speed-Reading Test

Read at your normal pace the following passage on memory by the author. Then calculate your reading speed in words per minute. The total number of words in the passage is approximately 1,300. Check the time as you start to read, and check it again as you finish; then divide 1,300 by the number of minutes you took to read the passage. This will give you your reading speed.

THE HISTORY OF MEMORY

From the time when man first began to depend on his mind for coping with the environment, the possession of an excellent memory has placed individuals in positions of both command and respect. The amazing feats in remembering accomplished by particular people were so impressive that they have become legendary.

THE GREEKS. It is difficult to say exactly when and where the first integrated ideas on memory arose. It is reasonable to state, however, that the first sophisticated concepts can be attributed to the Greeks some six hundred years before the birth of Christ.

As we look back on them now, these "sophisticated" ideas were surprisingly naive, especially since some of the men proposing them are numbered among the greatest thinkers the world has ever known.

In the sixth century B.C., Parmenides thought of memory as being a mixture of light and dark or heat and cold. He thought that as long as any given mixture remained unstirred, the memory would be perfect. As soon as the mixture was altered, forgetting occurred.

In the fifth century B.C., Diogenes of Apollonia advanced a different theory. He suggested that memory was a process which consisted of events producing an equal distribution of air in the body. Like Parmenides he thought that when this equilibrium was disturbed, forgetting would occur.

Not surprisingly, the first person to introduce a really major idea in the field of memory was Plato, in the fourth century B.C. His theory is known as the Wax Tablet hypothesis and is still accepted by some people today, although there is growing disagreement. To Plato the mind accepted impressions in the same way that wax becomes marked when a pointed object is moved around on its surface. Once the impression had been made, Plato assumed it remained until with time it wore away, leaving a smooth surface once more. This smooth surface was, of course, what Plato considered to be complete forgetting—the opposite aspect of the same process. As will become clear later, many people now feel that they are actually two quite different processes.

Shortly after Plato, Zeno the Stoic slightly modified Plato's ideas, suggesting that sensations actually "wrote" impressions on the wax tablet. When Zeno referred to the mind and its memory he did not place it in any particular organ or section of the body: "mind" was a loose and very unclear concept. The first man to introduce a more scientific terminology was Aristotle, in the late fourth century B.C. He maintained that the language previously used was not adequate to explain the physical aspects of memory. In applying his new language Aristotle attributed to the heart most of the functions that we properly attribute to the brain. Part of the heart's function, he realized, was concerned with the blood, and he felt that memory was based on the blood's movements. He thought forgetting to be the result of a gradual slowing down of these movements.

Aristotle made another important contribution to subsequent thinking on the subject of memory when he introduced his laws of the association of ideas. The concept of association of ideas and images is now generally thought to be of major importance to memory.

In the third century B.C., Herophilus introduced to the discussion "vital" and "animal" spirits. He theorized that the higher-order spirits produced the lower-order animal spirits, which included the memory, the brain, and the nervous system. All of these he thought to be secondary in importance to the heart.

It is interesting to note that one reason advanced by Herophilus for man's superiority over animals was the large number of creases in man's brain. (These creases are now known as convolutions of the cortex.) Despite the *fact* of his observation, Herophilus offered no *reason* for his conclusion. It was not until the nineteenth century, over two thousand years later, that the real importance of the cortex was discovered.

In summary, the Greeks made the following significant contribution: they were the first to seek a physical as opposed to a spiritual basis for memory; they developed scientific concepts and a language structure that helped the development of these concepts; and they contributed the Wax Tablet hypothesis, which suggested that memory and forgetting were opposite aspects of the same process.

THE ROMANS. Surprisingly, the contributions of the Romans were minimal. The major thinkers of their time, including Cicero in the first century B.C. and Quintilian in the first century A.D., accepted without question the Wax Tablet concept of memory, and did little further work.

Their major contribution was in the development of memory systems. It was they who first introduced the idea of a link system and a room system.

THE INFLUENCE OF THE CHRISTIAN CHURCH. The next major contributor to the progress of ideas on memory was the great physician Galen in the second century A.D. He located and delineated various anatomical and physiological structures, as well as further investigating the function and structure of the nervous system.

Like the later Greeks, he assumed that memory and mental processes were part of the lower order of animal spirits. These spirits he thought were manufactured in the sides of the brain, and it was consequently here that memory was seated.

Galen thought that air was sucked into the brain, mixing with the vital spirits. This mixture produced animal spirits which were pushed down through the nervous system, enabling us to feel and taste, etc.

Galen's ideas on memory were rapidly accepted and condoned by the Church, which at this time was beginning to exert a great influence. His ideas became doctrine, and on that account little progress was made in the field for fifteen hundred years. This mental suppression stifled some of the greatest minds that philosophy and science have produced.

St. Augustine in the fourth century A.D. accepted the Church's ideas, considering memory to be a function of the soul, which had a physical seat in the brain. He never expanded on the anatomical aspects of his ideas.

From the time of St. Augustine until the seventeenth century there were virtually no significant developments in ideas on memory, and even in the seventeenth century new ideas were restricted by doctrine.

Even such a great thinker as Descartes accepted Galen's basic ideas, although he thought that animal spirits were sent from the pineal gland on special courses through the brain until they came to the part where memory could be triggered. The more clear-cut these courses, the more readily, he thought, would they open when animal spirits traveled through them. It was in this way that he explained the improvement of memory and the development of what are known as "memory traces." A memory trace is a physical change in the nervous system that was not present before learning. The trace enables us to recall.

Another great philosopher who went along with the tide was Thomas Hobbes, who discussed and considered the idea of memory but had little to add to what had been said before. He agreed with Aristotle's ideas, rejecting nonphysical explanations of memory. He did not, however, specify the real nature of memory, nor did he make any significant attempts to locate it accurately.

In summary, it is evident from the theories of the sixteenth century intellectuals that the influence of Galen and the Church had been profound. Almost without exception these great thinkers uncritically accepted primitive ideas on memory.

Now that you have completed the reading, make your best recall notes on the passage you have just read. When you are making the notes, do not refer to the text. Also estimate, by percentage, your comprehension and recall.

The "average" score in such passages is a reading speed of about one hundred to three hundred words a minute, with a comprehension score of between 40 and 70 percent. The trained reader can often reach speeds well above six hundred words per minute, with virtually full comprehension. The ways in which this can be accomplished are outlined in this chapter.

When people make their "best recall notes" they often write them in the form of sentences or long phrases. The more advanced note-makers will concentrate their efforts on key phrases, and the exceptionally advanced will have concentrated their efforts in "key words." There are now new note-making techniques which go beyond even the best of these traditional note-making methods. (These new techniques are explained, with details and exercises for practice, in Chapter 6, on note-making and fast writing.)

The History of Speed Reading

Although speed reading can be traced to the beginning of this century, when the publication explosion swamped readers with more than they could possibly handle at normal reading rates, most early courses and information were based on information provided from a rather unexpected source—the air force.

Air force tacticians had noticed that a number of pilots were unable to distinguish, when flying, planes seen at a distance. In the life-and-death situation of combat, this inability was obviously an enormous disadvantage, and the air force psychologists and educationalists set about to remedy the situation. They developed a machine called a tachistoscope, which is simply a device for flashing images for varying instants of time on a large screen. They started by flashing fairly large pictures of friendly and enemy aircraft at very slow exposures and then gradually shortened the exposure while decreasing the size of the image seen. They found to their surprise that with training, the average person was able to distinguish almost specklike representations of different planes when the images had been flashed on the screen for only one five-hundreth of a second.

Reasoning that the perceptual ability of the eyes had been vastly underrated, they decided to transfer this information to reading. Using exactly the same device and process, they first flashed one large word for as long as five seconds on a screen, gradually reducing the size of the word and shortening the length of the flash. This they were able to

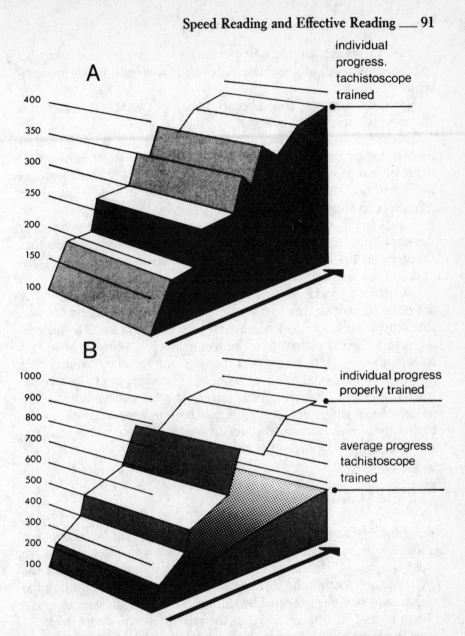

A

400
350
300
250
200
150
100

individual
progress,
tachistoscope
trained

B

1000
900
800
700
600
500
400
300
200
100

individual progress
properly trained

average progress
tachistoscope
trained

Traditionally, speed-reading schools gave their students graphs like A which were graded from 100 to 400. A small improvement therefore looked large. Reading ability should be measured on graphs reaching a maximum of 1,000 or more words a minute, like B. The improvement with tachistoscope training is small in comparison to what can be achieved with more efficient methods.

do until they were flashing four words simultaneously on a screen for one five-hundredth of a second, and were still able to obtain recognition.

As a consequence of this approach, most speed-reading courses and kits were based on tachistoscopic training.

This approach usually provided the student with a graph graded in units of ten from one hundred to four hundred words per minute (see figure). Most people, with regular training, were able to climb from an average of two hundred per minute to an average of four hundred per minute (also shown in figure). Unfortunately, the graduates of such training schemes reported a general dissatisfaction after a few weeks of "postgraduate reading." An enormous number of them noticed that shortly after the course had finished, their reading speed once again sank to their previous level.

Only recently was it realized that the *normal range* of reading ability is from roughly two hundred to four hundred words per minute and that most people operate at the lowest level of this range. The increasing reading ability observed in the tachistoscopic courses had in fact little to do with the tachistoscopic training, but was more a function of motivation being eked out over a period of weeks and of the readers' reaching the top of their normal range. Another explanation for the failure of the still-screen approach can be found by referring to the basic rule of observation: in order to see something clearly, the eye must be still in relation to the object it is seeing.

Basic Eye Movements

Because the words on the page are still, the eye must be still when it is looking at them, but because there are many words to read, the eye must also *move*. This apparently paradoxical situation, in which the eye is required both to be still and to move, is resolved by putting the two in sequence: the eye must be still to take in a single word or group of words, and then must move to the next group of words, where it must again be still, before moving on to the next word or group of words, and so on. The eye must therefore *primarily* be trained, not to see flashes, but to *move* efficiently.

The eye movements of the slow reader, complete with back-skipping, regression, and visual wandering off the page, are shown in the top diagram here. The lower diagram shows the eye movement of the more efficient reader, without back-skipping, regression, and wan-

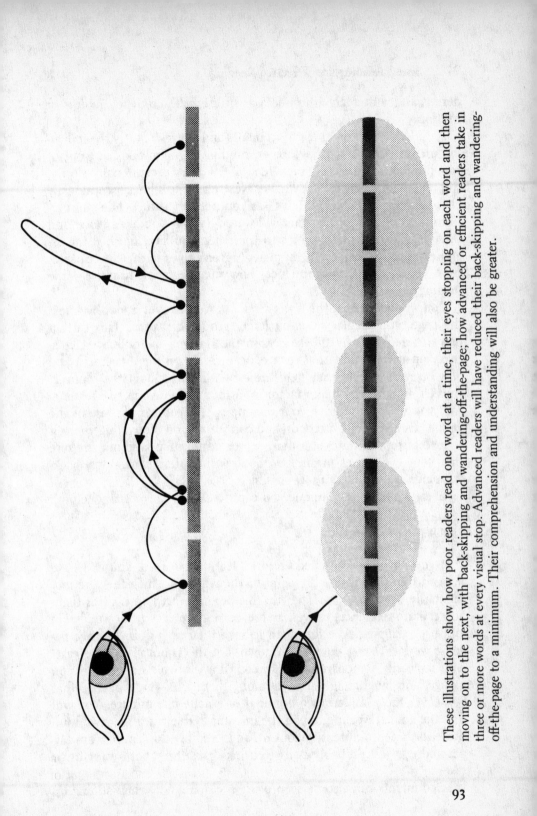

These illustrations show how poor readers read one word at a time, their eyes stopping on each word and then moving on to the next, with back-skipping and wandering-off-the-page; how advanced or efficient readers take in three or more words at every visual stop. Advanced readers will have reduced their back-skipping and wandering-off-the-page to a minimum. Their comprehension and understanding will also be greater.

dering, and with a larger number of words taken in for each "stop," or fixation.

In order to see how these movements and stops work, try the following exercise. Work with a partner, holding an open book in front of you just above eye level. First read a few lines exceptionally slowly, stopping on every word or syllable. Next read a few lines exceptionally fast, taking in as large "chunks" as you possibly can. While you perform this exercise your partner will watch the way your eyes move, and then describe the performance to you when you have finished the exercise. Once this has been completed, reverse roles so that you can see, from your partner's performance, how the eyes actually move while reading.

You will notice that the faster reader moves his eyes smoothly across the page with regular stops on larger groups of words. This further helps to explain why the tachistoscopic training methods were relatively unsuccessful. Rather than concentrating on the movement and flow of eye fixations, they held the eyes still throughout the training, thus eliminating the major factor in faster and more effective reading.

If you wish to improve your reading speed, you can dispose of the various tachistoscope methods, and concentrate on motivating yourself to read faster, taking two or more words per fixation, and making sure that your eye moves in an even flow, with as few regressions, back-skippings and wanderings as possible.

There is another technique you can use which is especially helpful.

Using a Visual Guide

If you have ever watched children learning to read, you will have noticed that they invariably point to the word on which they are momentarily concentrating. They do this because the pointer gives them an accurate reference, as well as preventing the eyes from wandering and back-skipping. We tell them to take their finger off the page because we feel that it slows them down, but this is not in fact the case. You can easily demonstrate this by counting off two hundred words on a page, and by guiding your eyes along them with your finger so that you cover the complete two hundred in exactly one minute. You will find the guide revealing to you the uncomfortable truth that two hundred words per minute is, to look at, an incredibly slow speed; your finger and eye will probably both feel held back; they both want to go faster.

Accountants can also be seen using a visual guide when adding up

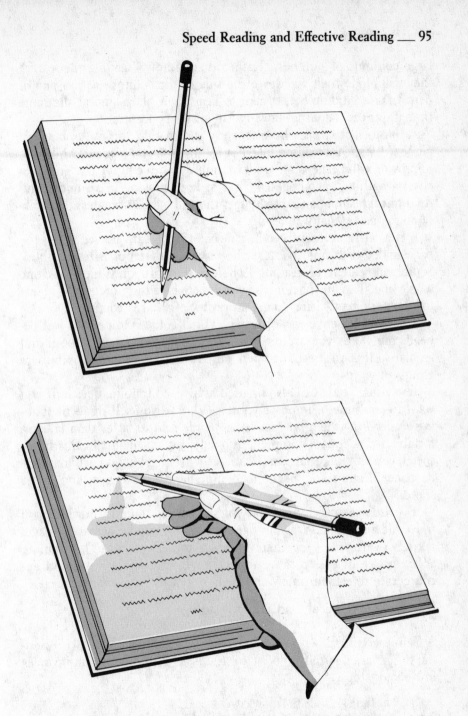

A visual guide improves reading efficiency. The guide should be long and thin like a pencil, and should be moved smoothly along either *over* the line being read or *underneath* it. The guide should be held slightly above the page.

large columns of numbers. Rather than simply "reading them off," they will guide their eye down the side of the columns with a pen or pencil. This guiding helps them to keep their place, and at the same time improves the visual flow and increases concentration.

A number of studies have recently shown that the use of a visual guide will increase reading speed by as much as 100 percent, while also improving comprehension, understanding, and memory. The guide focuses attention, encourages the eye to keep moving in a smooth and rhythmical fashion, and discourages the bad habits of regression, back-skipping, and visual wandering.

It is a far more useful reading device than a card moved down the page under each line, because the visual guide emphasizes the horizontal movement of reading, whereas the card only identifies one whole line. The print below the words being read is moreover left clear for the peripheral vision to get a preview of what is coming.

The most effective way of using a visual guide is to point it just beneath the words you are reading, keeping its movement smooth and regular so that your eyes can pick out, as they choose, the appropriate groups of words.

The visual guide can also be used as a speed training device. If you want to continue to improve your speed, give yourself frequent training sessions in which you move the guide a little faster than is comfortable for adequate comprehension. If you can maintain this faster speed, you will find that your brain, rather than giving up, will increase its concentration and begin to comprehend at the new and faster speed.

It is also worth occasionally trying superspeed training, in which you move the guide as fast as your hand can possibly move across the page, taking in with your eyes whatever odd glimpses you can. This training accustoms your eye to move exceptionally fast across print, and encourages it to establish new and higher "norms" for reading speed.

Reference, Technical, and Study Reading

Before getting down to the business of actually reading, it is essential to prepare yourself properly for the task. This preparation involves four major steps:

1. time
2. amount
3. knowledge
4. aims and goals

1. TIME. In Chapter 2, on memory, you saw how understanding, comprehension, and recall are vastly improved if your time is organized into reasonable learning units. This is especially important at the beginning of technical reading, for not only does it enable you to maximize recall and learning, it also enables you to make more sensible judgments about the amount you will be able to cover in the time period.

2. AMOUNT. Next, it is important to make a reasonable estimate of the amount to be covered in the time you have given yourself. While making this estimate, you should also break up the amount into reasonable units, corresponding with the units of time you have planned for yourself.

Preplanning the time and amount in this way gives you the psychological advantage of "knowing where you are going" rather than meandering off into a threatening and unknown territory, with no particular goal in sight.

3. KNOWLEDGE. In order to "tune up" your mind, it is advisable to do a brief review (two to five minutes) of any knowledge you already have which is relevant to what you are about to read. This establishes all the right connections in your brain, and makes it far more easy for you to pick up the new information that will be coming in. This can be especially important when reading up-to-date journals and papers, etc.

If the material you are reading is totally new, it is often advisable to go first to a reference book, such as an encyclopedia. This will give you an introductory overview of any new subject, giving your mind the necessary and basic hooks it needs to grapple with the new information.

4. AIMS AND GOALS. By setting yourself reasonable aims and goals, you can further tune up your mind for the task ahead. Jot down the questions you want answered from whatever you are about to read, and then read actively for the answers. You will find that if you have asked the right questions, even new material will seem somehow familiar, and your learning will be much easier.

The questions you set yourself, apart from being specifically directed to the aim you have in mind, should also include some that are as open-minded and as open-ended as possible. This open-minded and open-ended approach will help you to absorb new information and to avoid reading only what you want to read—an easily acquired habit of mind that tends toward a "funnel vision" approach to learning.

If you have difficulty in establishing your aims and goals, you can always start with those questions that children ask of their parents:

how
when
where
why
what
who
definitions

This series of questions, which I often call the "kids' kit," covers most of the important areas in any subject; for example: "when" picks out all items of historical importance, "who" hooks on to all the major people, and so on.

After having organized your time limit, chosen the amount and divided it into reasonable sections, and tuned up your mind by reviewing your present knowledge and establishing aims and goals, you are now more than prepared.

Applying Yourself to the Reading Task

At this stage, most people start "plowing through" from the first page, which is definitely not the most efficient way to read. A better way is similar to the way most people approach jigsaw puzzles.

Usually, people look at the picture on the box first, read the general instructions, and find out how many pieces there are in the entire puzzle. They then find a suitable place in which to do the puzzle, open the box, tip out the pieces, and turn them all right side up. They follow this by sorting out the edge and corner pieces and then arranging the pieces by general color areas. They select special areas, and begin to fill in. When coming across difficult pieces, they put them aside, waiting for a later stage when they will more easily fit them in.

The jigsaw approach can be most usefully applied to the reading of technical references, trade journals, management books, learned papers, and study texts, and should normally involve the following stages:

1. survey
2. preview
3. inview
4. review

1. SURVEY.   The purpose of the survey is to give you an outline of the material you are about to read. Check first to see if there is any summary or conclusion. If there is, read it first, for it gives you the kernel of what you are about to read. During the survey you should also cover, if they exist, the following items:

table of contents
photographs
graphs
number tables
marginal comments
footnotes
chapter headings
subheadings
glossaries
index

When you have finished this stage you will usually be able to decide whether you wish to read in greater depth. If you do, move on to the next stage.

2. PREVIEW.   The preview is similar to the survey, except that it is done on the text itself. When previewing, it is usually advisable to check the beginnings and ends of chapters, sections, and paragraphs. Many authors condense much of their information in these areas, and it is a quick and efficient way of further checking the general outline of a book.

During this stage you should place visible markers at the division points which mark your time periods, and on pages to which you may need to refer continually.

The preview, like the survey, might prove to be the last stage of your reading, especially if you find the material does not meet with your aims and goals, is of a level too difficult for you, or has already answered your questions.

3. INVIEW. The inview can be compared to the stage where you begin to fill in the jigsaw puzzle. During this stage you will normally be rooting more deeply for answers to your questions, and should be marking with a soft pencil on the margin those areas to which you wish to return, either because they are especially noteworthy or because they present you with momentary difficulty. *Do not* at this stage worry over difficulties. Leave them, as with the jigsaw puzzle, until the end.

4. REVIEW. This is your final stage, and at this point in your reading you should be checking that your aims and goals have been generally accomplished, reviewing what you have read, making final notes (for methods of making notes, see the next chapter), and planning your ongoing review and next study period.

It is important to realize that this approach is, above all things, *flexible*. A very difficult mathematics or physics book might require two or three surveys and two or three reviews. A light novel might require simply one skimmed reading. The book on which you wish to write a special paper or report might require a number of inviews, each with a different aim or goal in mind. Your technical journal might require a flip through or an in-depth study.

If you begin to approach reading in this way, you will find to your surprise and enjoyment that it becomes increasingly easy. The more you learn, the easier it will be to take in new knowledge, which means an automatic increase in reading speed. The increase in speed means that even more knowledge will be acquired and the positive spiral has begun.

Keys for Further Improvement

In addition to this general approach, there are a number of other useful things you can do to help you with your general reading:

1. SPEED. Before any reading do a quick "dash" over the print. This will both briefly accustom your eyes to higher speeds and ensure that they are "warmed up" for the reading task ahead.

2. TEMPERATURE.   For learning it is always best to have a slightly cool rather than a slightly warm temperature. 16–18° C (68–70° F) is ideal.

3. SURROUNDINGS.   Make sure that your surroundings are pleasant—but not *too* comfortable! Your learning area should preferably be free of anything which could distract you while you are reading.

4. EYE REST.   During extended reading periods, make sure that you regularly look up from the book and focus on distant objects. This relaxes and rests the muscles of the eyes, enabling you to carry on reading without unnecessary fatigue.

5. VISUALIZING.   Occasionally stop, close your eyes, and try to reproduce, in your mind's eye, a page of print or a photograph or graph that you have just looked at. Apart from providing a useful rest, this will significantly help to increase your recall, while providing useful training for your imagination.

6. POSTURE.   Your posture should be reasonably upright, but not rigid or tense. If it is correct, and if your desk or table surface is at a reasonable height, the distance between your eyes and book should be between fifteen and twenty-four inches.

These techniques can be supplemented with exercises outlined in the previous chapter. If you practice them regularly, your reading will become a far more enjoyable and much less tense experience.

SELF-CHECK 14—Check Yourself Again

When you have finished the *entire book,* return to this continuation of the essay on memory that you began earlier in this chapter, time yourself again, and calculate your words per minute (there are 1,300 words in this passage also). Afterward make your best recall notes in key words and patterns. (The technique of using key words and patterns is explained in the following chapter.) When you have completed this entire exercise, compare both results with your speed of reading and note-making in the initial reading exercise.

THE HISTORY OF MEMORY—continued

TRANSITIONAL PERIOD—THE EIGHTEENTH CENTURY. One of the first thinkers to be influenced by the new surge of science and by the ideas of Newton was David Hartley, who developed the vibratory theory of memory. Applying Newton's ideas on vibrating particles, Hartley suggested that there were memory vibrations in the brain which began before birth. New sensations modified existing vibrations in degree, kind, place, and direction. After influence by a new sensation, vibrations quickly returned to their natural state. But if the same sensation appeared again the vibrations took a little longer to return. This progression would finally result in the vibrations remaining in their "new" state, and a memory trace was established.

Other major thinkers of this period included Zanotti, who was the first to link electrical forces with brain functions, and Charles Bonnet, who developed the ideas of Hartley in relation to the flexibility of nerve fibers. He thought that the more often nerves were used, the more easily they vibrated and the better memory would then be.

The theories of these men were more sophisticated than previous ones because they had been largely influenced by developments in related scientific fields. This interaction of ideas laid the groundwork for some of the more modern theories of memory in the nineteenth century.

THE NINETEENTH CENTURY. With the progress of science in Germany in the nineteenth century, some important developments occurred. Many of the ideas initiated by the Greeks were overthrown, and work on memory expanded to include the biological sciences.

Prochaska finally and irrevocably rejected the age-old idea of animal spirits, on the ground that it has no scientific basis and no evidence to support it. He felt that limited existing knowledge made speculation on the location of memory in the brain a waste of time. "Spatial localization may be possible," he said, "but we just do not know enough at the moment to make it a useful idea." It was not for fifty years that localizing the area of memory became a useful pursuit.

Another major theory presented in this century was that of Marie-Jean-Pierre Flourens, who "located" the memory in *every* part of the brain. He said that the brain acted as a whole and could not be interpreted as an interaction of elementary parts. His views held the field of physiology for some time, and it is only recently that great strides have been made in the development of our thinking on memory.

MODERN THEORIES. Modern developments in memory have been aided to an enormous degree by advances in technology and methodology. Almost without exception psychologists and other thinkers in this field agree that memory is located in the cortex, which is the large area of the brain covering the surface of the cerebrum. Even today, however, the exact localization of memory areas is proving a difficult task, as is the accurate understanding of the function of memory itself.

Current thought has progressed from Hermann Ebbinghaus's work with learning and forgetting curves at the turn of the century to advanced and complex theories.

Research and theory can be roughly divided into three main areas: work on establishing a biochemical basis for memory; theories which suggest that memory can no longer be considered as a single process but must be broken down into divisions; and Wilder Penfield's work on brain stimulation.

Research into the biochemical basis for memory was initiated by Hyden in the late 1950s. This theory suggests that RNA (ribonucleic acid), a complex molecule, serves as a chemical mediator for memory.

RNA is produced by the substance DNA (deoxyribonucleic acid) which is responsible for our genetic inheritance—for example, DNA decides whether your eyes will be blue or brown.

A number of experiments have been performed with RNA, lending support to the idea that it does indeed have a lot to do with the way in which we remember things. For example, if animals are given certain types of training, the RNA found in certain cells is changed. And further, if the production of RNA in an animal's body is stopped or modified, these animals are unable to learn or remember.

An even more exciting experiment showed that when RNA was taken from one rat and injected into another, the second rat "remembered" things that he had never been taught, but that the first rat had.

While research into this aspect of memory is progressing, other theorists are saying that we should stop emphasizing "memory" and concentrate more on the study of "forgetting." It is their position that we do not so much remember as gradually forget.

Encompassing this idea is the duplex theory of remembering and forgetting which states that there are two different kinds of information retention: long-term and short-term. For example, you have probably experienced a different "feeling" in the way you recall a telephone number which has just been given to you, and the way you recall your own telephone number.

The short-term situation is one in which the idea is "in" the brain but has not yet been properly coded and is therefore more readily forgotten. In the long-term situation the idea has been completely coded, filed, and stored and will probably remain for years, if not for life.

Research into direct brain stimulation was initiated by Dr. Wilder

Penfield, a clinical surgeon. When performing craniotomies (removal of a small section of the brain) in order to reduce epileptic attacks, Penfield had first to remove a portion of the skull lying over the side of the brain. Before operating Penfield conducted a systematic electrical stimulation of the open brain, and the patient, who remained conscious, reported his experience after each stimulation. In an early case, Penfield stimulated the temporal lobe of the brain and the patient reported a recreated memory of a childhood experience.

Penfield found that stimulating various areas of the cortex produces a range of responses, but that only stimulation of the temporal lobes leads to reports of meaningful and integrated experiences. These experiences are often *complete* in that when recreated they include the color, sound, movement, and emotional content of the original experiences.

Of particular interest in these studies is the fact that some of the memories stimulated electrically by Penfield had been unavailable in normal recall. In addition to this, the stimulated experiences seemed to be far more specific and accurate than normal conscious recall, which tends to be a generalization. It is Penfield's belief that the brain records *every* item to which it pays conscious attention, and that this record is basically permanent, although it may be "forgotten" in day-to-day living.

That brings us roughly up to date. Looking back over history, we see that real thinking in this area has been going on for only a little over twenty-five hundred years, and that for as many as two thousand of those years virtually no advances were made. In fact, only a few hundred years of progressive thought have passed, and during those years man has progressed from thinking of memory in terms of spirits and vague concepts to tracking it down to a fairly small area of the body.

But even now, he is still only at the beginning of his search. Every month more than eighty new articles are published from the major research centers in the world. It may not be long before the next major advance is made.

6

Note-Making and Fast Writing

Concise and efficient note-making has been a problem for everyone who has gone through the normal school system. This chapter outlines traditional note-making methods and presents the latest evidence for the effectiveness of new key-word note-making techniques. In addition to this, advice is given on more creative and flowing note-making, as well as on abbreviation techniques and the solution of physical problems in fast writing.

KEY WORD SUMMARY

Traditional methods
Speed
Key words
Creative note-making
Abbreviation
The physical process

SELF-CHECK 15

Before reading on, complete the following exercise. Think back to the last book that you read, whatever type of book it was, and imagine that in one year's time you are going to lead a seminar discussion on that book. You know that you will be away for most of the time between now and the seminar, so you decide to make the most useful notes you can—your best recall notes. The purpose of these notes will be for you to take them out in a year's time, and on the basis of them to lead the seminar discussion. Give yourself up to half an hour for the exercise, and when you have completed it read on.

Comments on Self-Check 15   In self-check 15, 70 percent of people write paragraph and sentence "summaries" of the book. The remaining 30 percent use key phrases and key words, usually in some form of list order. Read on to find out how these approaches fare in note-taking studies for effectiveness, and how they compare with the new approaches.

Traditional Methods

Stenography, a term which used to cover only shorthand techniques, now covers a wide range of techniques devoted to getting essential information down in the most efficient way possible.

The most popular method to date has indeed been the shorthand system, which by abbreviating the symbols for letters and words enabled people to write as fast as they could speak. A number of people will learn shorthand for school, college, and university to ensure they miss none of the lecturer's words of wisdom.

Studies on Key Words

Recently, this approach has been strongly questioned, where the purpose of taking notes is learning and recall.

Dr. Gordon Howe at Exeter University and others have done repeated studies on different kinds of note-making, and have noticed an interesting trend which can be summarized in the rather paradoxical statement: notes yes, but the fewer the better. The different note-making techniques were, in reverse order of merit, ranked as follows:

1. no notes at all (the worse technique)
2. complete transcript notes given by the lecturer or teacher, etc.
3. complete transcript notes made by the person learning
4. summary sentence notes given by the lecturer or teacher
5. summary sentence notes made by the learner
6. key-word notes given by the lecturer or teacher
7. key-word notes made by the learner

In this last category it was also found that, within reason, the fewer key words, the better. Key words were defined as those which incorporated the most relevant sense in the shortest way possible, and which also were those words which gave the most immediate recall when the notemaker was tested. They were figuratively described by one student as being like the steppingstones one needs for a path over a swamp, the swamp being the mass of grammar-words which contain the key words, but which are themselves not essential for recall.

This finding was initially surprising, but after investigation the reason became clear. Our minds, despite what we have previously thought, do not basically recall in sentences, but in key words and images. Of the words we hear, speak, and see, only 1–10 percent are these essential key words.

To prove to yourself that your mind does not work basically with sentences, jot down on a spare piece of paper all the sentences of ten words or more that you can recall having spoken, read, or heard *during your entire lifetime*. (These should be general sentences, and not ones that you have purposely learned by repetition, such as songs and poetry.) Try this exercise before reading on.

You will probably find that you are able to get only a very few. Does it surprise you to learn, however, that the range of sentences you have encountered is numbered in the tens of millions?

Another exercise for checking on the way in which your brain works is to think about how, inside your head, your thoughts are organized when you are telling someone about a special event or circumstance. Do the sentences line up in long queues waiting to get out? No, you have in your mind pictures of the important objects, and key words, and around these you construct whatever sentences you need to express your thoughts.

Again, before reading on, go back to the previous chapter (see page 89), and check over your best recall notes. If you are like 90 percent of the population, you will probably have written these out neatly and in sentences. Knowing now that best recall notes are ideally in key words, take a colored pen or pencil and circle only those words which you now recognize as keys to your recall. When you have circled the key words, count the total number of words you wrote down, then add up the total number of key words you have finally selected. Work out the percentage by dividing the small number by the large number and multiplying by 100.

Creative Note-Making

Making key-word notes eliminates 90 percent of the unnecessary note-making, and thus improves your effective writing/note-making speed by as much as ten times. In addition to this advantage, your recall will also be greatly improved, because it will not have to waste time sifting through all the unnecessary words.

More advanced techniques can help you to recall even better. Referring to the information we discovered about our memory, we can use the fact that we recall things which are linked and things which are outstanding, to make notes which are many times more effective than even the best standard key-word notes.

Using arrows, colors, and special codes, you can make connections between your key words which immediately show you where the relationships lie. This is far superior to lines or lists of key words, which give you the essence but do not show you the relationship between the ideas.

To make these newly linked key words and images even easier to recall, you can make them outstanding.

This can be done in various ways, including:

> color
> three-dimensionalizing
> size variation
> outlining
> underlining

Making notes in this way will enable you to speed up even more, for you will not need as much repetition as even the best key-word notemaker sometimes finds necessary. These new notes will develop in front of you a mental map of information, improving all aspects of your mental performance.

By referring to the mind map at the end of chapter 1, you will find examples of the above techniques and will see how effective they are for assisting your recall.

Having reached a stage where your note-making gives the essence, and does not concern itself with unnecessary and irrelevant words, you will already be a far "speedier" note-maker than the average. You can increase this ability even more by using some of the techniques that originally inspired formal shorthand writing.

Abbreviations

Knowing that the words you have are essential, you can begin to abbreviate even these. One of the most effective methods is to write the word without vowels, and using only the consonants. It is surprising how readily your eye will recognize the outline. Fr xmpl I m sr y wll hv no dffclty rdng ths bbrevtn.

Physically Speeding Up

You can speed up your writing by giving yourself practice sessions at writing faster. The average writer can record somewhere between twenty-five and thirty-five five-letter words per minute. If you give yourself one-minute practice "speed sessions" you will find that you can considerably improve on this.

To achieve increased speed and maintain it over long periods of time, you must avoid the danger of writer's cramp and muscular tension. A reasonably relaxed and upright posture is far better than the scrunched-up hunch-shouldered collapse that many of us get ourselves into. In addition, as with other areas mentioned in this book, it is far better to have a smooth regular flow of activity than to have an occasional muscularly tense and more rigid spurt.

Extending Your Note-Making

One exciting aspect of this new form of patterning notes is that it allows you to develop other mental areas in addition to recall. This applies particularly to developing your creative, organizational, and presentation abilities. It is on these areas that the next chapter concentrates.

7

Creativity

Most people possess a much greater creative ability than they have ever thought possible. This chapter, referring to Chapters 1 and 2 on the brain and on memory, indicates that traditional methods of testing creativity are inadequate. New explanations for creative thinking are given, and an original approach to creative thinking is touched on in the mind-map section.

KEY WORD SUMMARY

Self-estimates
A creativity test
Standard interpretations
Brain structure
Memory
Standard testing
Two aspects
Exercise
Mind maps

SELF-CHECK 16

A. Circle the term which best describes your creativity level:

    Superior   Excellent   Above average   Average

          Below average   Poor   Terrible

B. On a scale of 0–100 (100 = highest), how would you rate yourself as a creative thinker?

                  _____

                      (0–100)

Interestingly, the "average" person rates himself or herself as below average on this test! On the scale of 0–100 the average lies between 60 and 85, considerably higher than in the listening self-estimates.

Now move on to the next self-check, which will enable you to score your ability to generate creative ideas against a psychometric norm:

SELF CHECK 17—A Creativity Test

On a separate piece of paper, give yourself *exactly two minutes* to write down, as fast as you can, all the different uses you can think of for an ordinary paper clip. When you have finished the exercise, and *only* when you have finished, continue reading.

Score this test by adding up the total number of uses thought of, and dividing by 2 to give you an average number of uses thought of per minute. (The average score ranges between 2 and 8.) It is a standard test given in schools, universities, and large business organizations to determine "inherent creative capacity." After reading the following information about creativity you will realize that your inherent creative capacity is far greater than this simple test could possibly measure, and that there are easy and relaxing ways of releasing your potential.

The average universal score on the alternate-uses test (after you have divided by 2) is 4; 8 is an unusually high score, and 12 very rare indeed. A score of 16 makes you better than one in a thousand. Can you improve your score, and if so by how much?

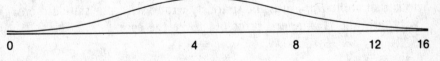

| 0 | 4 | 8 | 12 | 16 |

Creativity and Your Brain's Structure

Creativity, of all the mental areas, is the one in which most people rank themselves especially low. This is not surprising, because as you have realized from the chapter on the use of the brain, the "creative brain," for want of a better expression, is generally left out of education. Any activity which involves imagination, color, rhythm, or form has been traditionally frowned upon as "less intelligent." Fortunately we now have more information to work with, and creativity can be seen as a necessary part of a well-balanced education and personality.

The Fallacy of Standard Testing

The test in which you were asked to think of as many uses as you could for a paper clip is one of the traditional tests given to measure this aspect of your intellect. The faults of this test were of two main kinds. First, it assumed creative ability to be simply quantitative—i.e., dependent on the *number* of uses a person could think of; and second, even in the quantitative area it was weak. It did not actually measure the "basic or innate" capacities that it purported to measure—that is, creativity. Instead it measured how inadequately the brain had been taught to combine language and imagination.

The irrelevance of this test can be seen by picturing an imaginary brain salesman who is trying to convince an audience that they must "buy brains." He tells them he has the most amazing product ever and he has three pieces of information, all academically valid, that will convince them they must buy.

First he explains the physiology of the brain in detail, closing on the emphatic point that the number of patterns that can be formed in any single brain is 1 followed by 10,000,000 kilometers of zeros.

Second, he points out that the simple mnemonic memory techniques show that the human brain can link any object with any other object; for if it could not, these systems, which worked for centuries, would immediately fail.

And third, he states that his fantastic product can, when put under pressure, think of as many as six uses for a paper clip in a minute!

When these three facts are placed next to each other, it becomes obvious that *something* must be seriously wrong with our standard creativity test, and this indeed turns out to be the case.

The Quantitative Aspect of Creativity

All that the test measures is the rigidity with which the person being tested has been taught to use language, especially words like "uses." The more rigidly taught mind will assume that "uses" refers to ordinary, sensible applications of a paper clip. The less rigidly taught mind, and the one which consequently will be regarded as more creative, will find more expansive interpretations of the word "uses," and consequently will come up with many more applications for the paper clip.

The creative genius will break all the ordinary boundaries, and will include in his list many "far out" applications such as melting a few billion of them down to form the shell of a spaceship.

The creative mind is expanding his connections for the word "uses" to include the phrase "connections with."

So that you can prove this for yourself, forty items have been listed below for you to associate with the concept "paper clip." When you, or you and your friends, have completed this series of associations, see if there is anything else in the universe you can think of which you or a friend cannot in some way or other connect with the idea of a paper clip.

orange	ear	glass	tea
watch	potato	chair	tree
window	kitchen	garden	house
leaf	pigeon	Germany	wine
table	bottle	wood	maid
radio	shoe	rain	newspaper
light bulb	book	water	pub
handbag	cup	holiday	banana
pen	cloud	dinner	mirror
tire	pepper	garage	cat

For some of these you will be able to find connections immediately; others may at first seem obscure and impossible. In the end you will find they can all be connected to "paper clip" in some way, as did the person who connected them all except "pigeon." This he was convinced had no connection, until a friend suggested using a paper clip to fix an important message onto the pigeon's leg.

If you have difficulty with any of the following, check the suggestions made by my students following the list.

Alternate Uses

1. Orange — The paper clip could be used to peel the orange or to stick a hole in the top so that you could drink the juice through the hole, or you could even have an orange paper clip.

2. Watch — The paper clip could be used to mend a watch or to replace one of the hands, or could be straightened out and placed in the earth to act as a sundial.

3.	Window	A paper clip made of glass could be melted down and made into the window of a doll's house.
4.	Leaf	A paper clip could be extended, sharpened at the tip, fixed to the end of a stick, and used as a park worker's device for spearing fallen leaves.
5.	Table	A gigantic paper clip could be variously bent to form an art nouveau table.
6.	Radio	A radio is simply a receiver of certain sound waves, designed to pick them up and transmit them. A large paper clip could be made of the appropriate materials and easily converted into a radio.
7.	Light bulb	A tungsten paper clip could be used as the filament for your light bulb.
8.	Handbag	A paper clip could be used as the clip to keep the bag closed, or could be used to attach the strap to the bag itself.
9.	Pen	Appropriately pointed, your paper clip, when dipped in ink, could easily be used as a writing instrument.
10.	Tire	A paper clip could be used to pick stones and gravel out of the tire's tread, or could be used to let air out of the tire if it is overinflated.
11.	Ear	A paper clip could be used for cleaning it, gently. . . .
12.	Potato	An extended paper clip could be used to pierce the potato, acting as a transmitter of heat, thus allowing you to cook the potato more efficiently.
13.	Kitchen	See item 12.
14.	Pigeon	A paper clip could be used to attach the identification tag to a pigeon's leg, or in the case of carrier pigeons to attach the desired message.
15.	Bottle	A paper clip turned into a spiral could be used as a corkscrew.
16.	Shoe	A paper clip could be used as an emergency substitute for a broken shoelace, or could be

used to remove dirt from any of the shoe's crevices.

17. Book — As a marker.

18. Cup — A large paper clip could be sculpted into a cup, and a small one could be sculpted into a drinking receptacle for a pet insect.

19. Cloud — Granulated paper clips could be used to seed the clouds in order to produce rain.

20. Pepper — A paper clip could be used to unclog your pepper shaker.

21. Glass — See item 3.

22. Chair — See item 5.

23. Garden — A paper clip could be used as a tool, or as the holder for identification tags on your exotic plants.

24. Germany — A paper clip could be used to pinpoint the country on a map.

25. Wood — Many paper clips are made of wood.

26. Rain — See item 19.

27. Water — A paper clip could be used to transfer water drop by drop in a delicate operation.

28. Holiday — In view of all previous uses thought of for paper clips, you should definitely take them on holiday!

29. Dinner — See items 12 and 13.

30. Garage — Paper clips should always be kept in your garage as a spare creative tool.

31. Tea — A paper clip could be used to hold together a broken tea bag.

32. Tree — A paper clip could be sculpted (and has been) into a model tree.

33. House — Most modern houses contain hundreds of them.

34. Wine — See item 15.

35. Maid — Use your imagination!

36. Newspaper — The paper clip can be used to clip newspaper clippings together, or, when straightened out

and made into a little cutter, to cut out articles of interest.

37. Pub   See item 15.

38. Banana   A paper clip could be used to peel the banana, or it could be made into a little hook from which a bunch of bananas could be hung.

39. Mirror   See item 3.

40. Cat   A gigantic wooden paper clip could be used as a scratching post for a cat, or a standard metal one could be used as a clip for an identification tag.

Once you realize this almost limitless quantitative creative ability, you may be able to write as many uses for a paper clip as your hand can physically write in a minute. This will mean that the test is measuring not your creative ability, but your writing speed.

If you are allowed to speak your answers, you can generate up to two hundred in a minute, and once again the test would not be measuring your creative power, simply your ability to speak at speed.

At this stage, when you are producing 200 or more uses per minute, in comparison to the average of between two and eight, it becomes obvious that far more information about the complex operations of our brains will be needed before we can assume that we know enough to measure even *one* aspect of its extraordinary capacities.

The Qualitative Aspect of Creativity

Apart from the quantitative side of creativity, there is another side generally omitted from tests like the one discussed. The second area of creativity is the qualitative. This includes such things as order, relevance, simple connectivity, complex connectivity, and an overall sense of completeness and harmony.

The qualitative aspect of creativity can be very well expressed in the brain-pattern form introduced in the previous chapter. If you wish to generate a large number of ideas, while at the same time giving them order and form, the brain pattern allows you to do this with exceptional ease, permitting you to organize, as well as to recall completely, your own personal "brainstorming" session. It can also be done in a group.

An Exercise in Creativity

In the center of a page draw an image of the thing around which you wish to generate your creative ideas. Working with speed uppermost in your mind, branch off from the center, connecting ideas wherever they "fit in" as fast as they come into your head.

When doing this activity, it is best to keep a single word per line, as each word has its own massive series of associations and if kept separate will tend to "spark off" more ideas and images than it will do if trapped in a phrase or sentence. Images and words on the branches near the center are usually the primary ideas, and the less primary ideas branch out toward the boundary of your pattern. Sometimes, however, you will notice that a given idea or image pops up all over the place at the extremes, and because of this omni-presence you will realize that it is perhaps the underlying concept with which you are really concerned.

It is also important when generating these ideas to print the letters separately. This is because your eye will be able to see them far more immediately than if they are in connected handwriting. In this speedy generation of ideas the advantage of immediate and clear vision will outweigh the disadvantage of the slightly longer time taken for printing.

Mind Maps

From this chapter you will by now realize that the way to prepare and organize your thoughts for most purposes is not in sentence or list form. The most appropriate way is to use a creative mind map, for not only will the ideas generated be far more numerous, they will also automatically fall into their own connected and sensible order.

By referring to the mind map at the end of chapter 1, you will find examples of the above techniques and will see how effective they are for assisting your recall.

The Great Minds

Not coincidentally, virtually all of the great brains in history used their creative imaginations as the foundation for their genius.

The example of Einstein in Chapter 1 is further confirmed by the knowledge that he actually invented, for himself, imagination games in which he would purposely take different ideas and creatively associate them in the manner outlined in the paper-clip exercise. He was constantly requesting others to join him in the expansion of this aspect of their minds.

Kekulé, a physical chemist, won the race to discover the structure of the benzene ring by using his creative imagination. After his days in the laboratory he would go home and sit in front of the fire, half awake, half asleep, letting the patterns of the flames and coals inspire him. He explained:

> I turned my chair to the fire and dozed. Again the atoms were gamboling before my eyes. This time the smaller groups kept modestly in the background. My mental eye, rendered more acute by repeated visions of this kind, could now distinguish larger structures, in manifold conformation; long rows sometimes more closely fitted together, all turning and twisting in snakelike motion. But look! What was that? One of the snakes had seized hold of its own tail and the form whirled mockingly before my eyes. As if by a flash of lightning I awoke.

He awoke with the structure of the benzene ring etched in his mind, and as a consequence, like Einstein, constantly urged his colleagues to "learn to dream, gentlemen."

History is filled with similar examples of great minds using their associative capacities in conjunction with their imaginations to produce the great mental leaps forward and new paradigms for the human race.

And in the modern world virtually every brainstorming and creative thinking group and think-tank structure is based on the active search for new associations and more and more creative imagination.

By using the information you have gathered from this chapter, in conjunction with the information on the left and right side of your brain and the information on mnemonic memory, you can easily join the community of creative thinkers.

Numeracy

Although many people have a fear of numbers, the latest information on the brain indicates that everyone has an enormous basic mathematical ability. Part of this research has shown that your brain divides work between the mathematical side and the nonmathematical side. The bulk of this chapter deals with special and easier ways of handling addition, subtraction, multiplication, and division.

KEY WORD SUMMARY

Fear
Basic capacity
Your brain and mathematics
Addition
Subtraction
Multiplication
Division
Enjoying mathematics

Fear of Numbers

"Mathematics," "calculation," "algebra," "fractions," "long division," "subtraction," multiplication," "addition," and many other similar words referring to the world of numbers, give little twinges of fear to more than half the people who hear them.

Why? It is fortunately not because we have a basic inability in this area, but because we have been "trained away" from mathematics. At school, the mathematical subjects are often described as "academic," "difficult," and "only for the real brains." In the early stages many children become bored very quickly with reciting tables over and over again, and many others, having failed over some of their first calculations, assume that they are "no good" at it and concentrate on other subjects.

Adding to the problems that we have with mathematics is our assumption that numbers are a particularly male domain. In many schools, girls were actively discouraged from going on with mathematics, a decision that certainly placed them at a disadvantage and that was based on superstition and assumption rather than on fact.

Your Amazing Latent Mathematical Capacity

We now know that there are four main factors which determine mathematical ability, and these are based not on race or sex, but on:

1. techniques
2. practice
3. memory
4. brain's basic ability

1. TECHNIQUES. Over the years mathematicians have developed increasingly easy techniques for dealing with different forms of mathematical calculation. These are now more readily available, and those who use them are inevitably better "calculators" than those who do not. This chapter outlines, with examples, some of the more basic techniques.

2. PRACTICE. All good calculators, especially those considered "great," admitted that their skill was achieved not only by techniques but also by continual practice—none was just "able to juggle with numbers." As with other mental areas, the ability to calculate is a skill, and requires practice to enable the brain to become familiar with the various aspects of the task.

3. MEMORY. Without exception, the great calculators committed to memory many of the fundamental techniques and formulae necessary to their art. Previously, this was seen as an insurmountable barrier by those who thought that the memory had a limited capacity. As you will now have learned from the chapter on memory, each one of us has an almost limitless memory, and if your memory is used properly it will find all memory tasks relatively easier, including mathematics.

4. THE BRAIN'S BASIC ABILITY.   In the same way as we in the past underestimated the capacity of memory, so we underestimated the general ability of the brain. It was assumed that some people were
basically capable in mathematics, and that others were not, no matter
how much assistance they were given. What we now know, of course,
is that the brain has an almost limitless capacity, and that this ranges
over all the subjects, including the "sciences" and "arts." Professor
Ornstein's research on the left and right halves of the brain has also
shown that each of us has a "mathematical" brain and an "imaginative" brain, and that our potential in each is basically equal. Any "disability" that we may have is probably due to our leaving that area
untended, rather than to any basic fault in the working of the brain.

Weakness in mathematics may also stem from early ability being
dampened. One six-year-old boy, for example, was always able in his
mathematics class to give the teacher answers to math questions the
minute the teacher had finished asking. The boy never wrote anything
down, and as a consequence was told that what he was doing was
"wrong." He thought about this for a few days, and came into the class
saying that he used "moon numbers" to do the calculations in his
head. Moon numbers, it turned out, was his name for special numbers
that he used to reduce other large numbers to more simple units. He
would then juggle with the simple units, converting the final unit to a
large number which gave him the correct answer. He called them
"moon numbers" because someone had told him about the solar system and the stars, and he thought that if the numbers were "wrong"
they must have come from outside the earth. He was eventually pres-
sured to stop using them, as parents complained that the entire class
was being dragged along too fast and the other children were unable to
keep up.

These four "qualifications" for becoming a good calculator indicate
that virtually everyone can do it. If anyone is still in doubt, and insists,
"I know that I would never be able to do calculation and mathematics," it should be pointed out that if they could not do mathematics
they would not be alive. For our brains are doing the most incredible
series of mathematical calculations and computations during nearly
every second of the day.

During every waking moment your eyes are "calculating" with millions of tiny bits of light information. These bits of information continually add, subtract, blend, and multiply, depending on your
attention, motivation, and state of general awareness.

Simultaneously, that part of the brain which handles your hearing is mathematically discriminating between the millions of different nuances in sound, while also working on a complicated formula that adds and multiplies the intensity of the sound waves in order to give you an idea of loudness.

While all of this is going on, your brain is making sure that the number of electrochemical reactions in your brain every moment (a number between 100,000 an 100,000,000) is perfectly balanced, while also calculating that the number of heartbeats and breaths per minute is exactly right for the body's fuel and energy needs.

And finally, while all of *that* is going on, you may be choosing for yourself the largest portion of pie (an instantaneous geometrical calculation of a three-dimensional object's size and volume in space) and eating it (an activity which requires your brain to calculate the weight, volume, velocity, and direction of yet another three-dimensional object in space, making sure that it is directly on target).

When you consider all this, it becomes obvious that everyone is "good at mathematics" whether he or she likes it or not. So rather than wasting time on false premises and fears, let us get on with the job of showing your brain, which *can* do it, how to deal with some of the basic techniques for improving its mental arithmetic and its ability to add, subtract, multiply, and divide.

An Example of Quick Calculation   If you wish to subtract a number from a number such as 100, 1,000, 10,000, 100,000, and 1,000,000, *do not* work from the right in the traditional manner.

Work from the *left* to the *right*, subtracting each individual number from 9, and the last one from 10.

For example, if you want to subtract 76 from 100, you take 7 from 9, which is 2; and 6 from 10, which is 4, giving the correct answer: 24.

If we want to subtract 527 from 1,000, we work from the left, subtracting 5 from 9, which is 4; 2 from 9, which is 7; and 7 from 10, which is 3, giving us 473.

If we wish to subtract 792 from 10,000, we subtract 0 from 9, which is 9; 7 from 9, which is 2; 9 from 9, which is 0; and 2 from 10, which is 8, giving again the correct answer: 9,208.

As you can see, you subtract the lower number only from the zeros, and not from the 1. If your lower number is much smaller than the large number, then you add zeros to the lower number until it reaches the farthest-left zero of the high number, as we did in the last calculation, which was taking 0792 from 10,000.

Another way of looking at this method is to say that when subtracting from, say, 1,000 we change that number to 999 for the moment, then finally add 1 to compensate.

9	9	9	9
−0	−7	−9	−2
9	2	0	7
			+1
9	2	0	8

With only a minimum amount of practice you can develop this mental arithmetic into an almost instant answer, and can often, if challenged by others, get to the stage of giving them the answer almost as they give you the question.

Try this technique both by writing your numbers and answers down, and then by doing them "in your head."

Addition

Among the many techniques for addition, there are four which make the basic process considerably easier:

1. 10-packets
2. complete 10s
3. multiples
4. splitting the numbers

10-PACKETS. Whenever adding long columns of numbers, always look for the "10-packets." For example, when adding

57
58
33
91
72
46
19
64

it is a waste of time to add them up by mumbling to yourself 9 plus 4 is 13, plus 6 is 19, plus 2 is 21, plus 1 is 22, and so on.

It is far easier to link the numbers that make 10, giving you a series of 10-packets.

By quickly and lightly striking through the 10-packets with a pencil, you do not lose track of the ones you have already packeted. Thus in the column we are considering, the 7 and the 3 make a 10, the 8 and the 2 make a 10, the 1 and the 9 make a 10, and the 6 and 4 make a 10, giving us an easy calculation of 40. In the next column the 5 and the 5 make a 10, the 3 and the 7 make a 10, the 9 and the 1 make a 10, and the 4 and the 6 make a 10, which when we add the 4 from the other column gives us 440.

Try it with the next addition problem:

```
93
28
32
86
61
17
44
22
```

In the units column the 3 and the 7 make a 10, the 8 and the 2 make a 10, and the 6 and the 4 make a 10, giving three tens with 3 left over: 33. In the next column the 9 and the 1 make a 10, the 8 and the 2 make a 10, and the 6 and the 4 make a 10 with 5 left over, to which we add the 3 from the previous column, giving a total of 383.

Putting numbers in 10-packets can often double the speed of your calculations.

COMPLETE 10s.   You take the 10-packet technique one step further by combining two-digit numbers that form multiples of 10. This technique can be seen clearly from the following example:

```
34
26
97
15
13
55
```

By blending these in an easy manner, we can break this column down into: 34 and 26 make 60; 97 and 13 make 110; 15 and 55 make 70. Then 60 plus 110 plus 70 equals 240.

As with 10-packets, this technique can often reduce by one half the time you spend on a lengthy calculation.

MULTIPLES.   When you are faced with a long column of numbers, it is often useful to check down the entire column, seeing how many numbers there are which are repeated. Your addition problem can then be made simpler by applying the multiplication tables to what initially appeared to be a large and threatening addition problem.

For example:

7
8
6
1
5
7
7
9
6
5
1
5
9
9
8
7
8

Lightly marking off the numbers which are repeated, we find that there are three 9s, three 8s, four 7s, two 6s, three 5s, and two 1s. The problem can therefore be written out in this form:

$$3 \times 9 = 27$$
$$3 \times 8 = 24$$
$$4 \times 7 = 28$$
$$2 \times 6 = 12$$
$$3 \times 5 = 15$$
$$2 \times 1 = 2$$

The addition then becomes a far simpler one, and the correct answer of 108 is more easily found.

The example given here is a fairly short addition problem, but the more numbers there are to be added, the more useful becomes the technique of multiples.

SPLITTING THE NUMBERS.   Suppose you were given the following addition problems:

$$
\begin{array}{cc}
31 & 425 \\
\underline{54} & \underline{379}
\end{array}
$$

You could accomplish them by mental arithmetic if you "split the numbers." All that this implies is that you separate the numbers into two smaller parts, making a "hard" addition comparatively easy. Once you have done this the addition can be done with amazing simplicity.

In the first example we split the numbers 31 and 54:

$$
\begin{array}{cc}
3 & 1 \\
\underline{+5} & \underline{+4} \\
8 & 5
\end{array}
$$

Seen like this the answer 85 is more immediately obvious.

This splitting-the-number technique becomes even more useful with larger numbers. In the second example, again we split them into two more easily manageable numbers:

$$
\begin{array}{cc}
42 & 5 \\
\underline{+37} & \underline{+9} \\
79 & 14 \\
\underline{+1} & \\
80 &
\end{array}
$$

The first simple addition gives us 14, from which we carry the 1 to the other addition. The two additions combine to give the answer, 804.

Splitting the numbers, especially when applied to more difficult additions, can improve your speed of calculation, often by as much as five times. This technique and the others can all be improved by special practice and in particular by enjoyable "mathematical games" which lead to ever-increasing facility and enjoyment with numbers. A few of these are outlined at the end of the chapter.

Subtraction

There are two main techniques for making subtraction easier:

1. add
2. splitting the numbers

ADD.   Take an example like the following:

7596
4779

Most people will go through a process something like: "9 from 6 won't go, borrow, 9 from 16 is 7, carry the 1," and so on. Rather than performing what in the end could be a fairly laborious process, it is far easier to apply addition to the subtraction problem. Before you start, "prepare" the numbers in the following way. If a number above is smaller than the number below, you automatically add 10 to it and add 1 to the lower figure in the next column to the left. The subtraction is then done by reciting the number you need to add to each lower number in order to make up the number above it.

Thus in the example given, the subtraction will be done in the following way: the 5 and the 6, being smaller than the 7 and the 9, will be made into 15 and 16:

7	15	9	16
5	7	8	9

Speaking the answer to yourself as you go, you will recite: "9 plus 7 is 16, 8 plus 1 is 9, 7 plus 8 is 15, 5 plus 2 is 7."

By using this method you will have arrived at the correct answer, 2,817, in a more rapid manner than by the traditional method.

In long subtractions, you can save an enormous amount of time with this approach of preparing the number before you start to subtract and then "adding" to find the correct answer.

SPLITTING THE NUMBERS.   As with addition, subtraction can also be done more easily if larger numbers are split up into smaller ones. Imagine that you are given the following subtractions:

$$
\begin{array}{ccc}
97 & 154 & 528 \\
-32 & -42 & -212
\end{array}
$$

In the first example we split the numbers 97 and 32 into:

$$
\begin{array}{cc}
9 & 7 \\
-3 & -2 \\
\hline
6 & 5
\end{array}
$$

Seen like this the answer 65 is once again more immediately obvious.
    The two more "difficult" examples can be similarly split up, and it can be seen that the answers are almost immediately available.

$$
\begin{array}{cc}
15 & 4 \\
-4 & -2 \\
\hline
11 & 2
\end{array}
$$

$$
\begin{array}{cc}
52 & 8 \\
-21 & -2 \\
\hline
31 & 6
\end{array}
$$

In subtractions where the lower number has individual numbers in it that are larger than the individual number they are being taken away from, simply make the appropriate adjustments of adding 10s and giving 1s to the next column when splitting the numbers. To subtract 247 from 393, prepare the numbers like this:

$$
\begin{array}{cc}
39 & 13 \\
25 & 7 \\
\hline
14 & 6
\end{array}
$$

OTHER METHODS.   In addition to adding and splitting, there are other techniques in subtraction which you may explore in specialist books written on rapid calculation. The technique for quick calculation mentioned earlier in the chapter is an example of one of these more advanced approaches.

Multiplication

In multiplication there are two especially useful techniques:

1. multiplying by 5
2. multiplying by 11

MULTIPLYING A NUMBER BY 5. To multiply a number by 5 we multiply by 10 and then divide by 2. So to multiply 5 times 84,580 we simply add a zero (which is the same as multiplying by 10) to get 845,800; then we divide by 2 to get the answer, 422,900.

This method saves a lot of time and is even more useful when combined with the "group vision" technique for dividing numbers, as explained in the division section below.

MULTIPLYING A NUMBER BY 11. To multiply a two-digit number by 11, add the two digits together and put their sum in the middle.

For example, if we want to multiply 72 by 11, we split the 7 and 2 and put in the middle the sum of 7 and 2: 9, giving us 792 as the answer.

If the sum of the digits comes to 10 or more, simply add 1 to the left digit. For example, if we wanted to multiply 85 by 11 we would split the 8 and the 5, add them to give 13, giving us the answer 935.

In the same way that this technique suddenly becomes easy, so there is an enormous range of quick-calculation techniques for multiplying longer numbers by 11, multiplying numbers by 15, 25, 50, 75, 125, and others. And for those who are exceptionally interested, there are also techniques for the cross-multiplication of large numbers.

From the simple devices so far exemplified, it should be increasingly clear that mathematical ability depends on knowing how to do it—and there *are* methods.

Division

Two easy methods immediately present themselves for:

1. division by 2
2. division by 5

DIVISION BY 2.   To divide numbers by 2, apply "group vision." This means splitting the number into easily manageable sections, as we did with addition and subtraction. For example, to divide the number 6,728,544 by 2 we simply split it up in the following way:

6   72   8   54   4

Each of these numbers is easily divisible by 2, and running through them in order we get the answer 3, 36, 4, 27, 2: 3,364,272.

This little example indicates that anyone who wishes to become a rapid calculator must learn to scan numbers before getting involved too deeply in them. When you are dividing by 2, split up the number by means of small strokes or dashes—although as you progress you will normally find that a look will be sufficient. This group vision, while applying in particular to division by 2, is also a useful general principle in quick calculation.

DIVISION BY 5.   To divide any number by 5, divide by 10 and double it.

For example, 823 divided by 5 equals 82.3 multiplied by 2, equals 164.6.

As with the other mathematical procedures, there are many different techniques for dividing. The ones shown here are simply indications of the easier path that is available.

Keys for Continued Self-Improvement

As well as specific calculating techniques, there are a number of aids which will help to improve your ability with numbers:

1. READING WITH A GUIDE.   If you have ever seen an expert mathematician or accountant adding columns of numbers, you will have noticed that he guides his eyes down the columns by use of either his finger or a pencil. Sophisticated calculators use the guide because it helps their eyes maintain direction and concentration, as well as helping to maintain a more effective "group vision." Whenever you are doing calculation, it is advisable to use such a guide, preferably a pencil which will enable you to make appropriate markings.

2. IMAGINE.   The great calculators have emphasized that when performing their calculations they try to stop themselves from muttering, mumbling, or mentally sounding the numbers. Their technique is always to "see" the numbers and answers in their mind's inner eye. This technique takes a little time to improve, but always works. Referring to the chapter on the makeup of your brain, you will see that the calculators are using the "right side" of their brains to imagine the correct answer more clearly. Practicing in this way, therefore, has the advantage of enabling you to calculate very quickly and at the same time is a useful exercise for developing the mental abilities of your right brain.

3. PLAYING MATHEMATICAL GAMES.   Three useful games for sharpening up your mental calculating ability are the "Hundred Complement" and the "Double" and the "Half" games.

You say "Hundred Complement" to your partner and throw him 68; he then has to throw back 32. Then he throws a number under 100 to you—for example, 26—and you have to throw back 74. There are all kinds of ways of scoring such a game, although it can be better not to score at all but simply to enjoy the back-and-forth excitement of increasing speed.

The "Double" and "Half" games are similar. You throw the number 33, and your opponent has to throw back 66. He throws 95, and you have to throw back 190. Or you throw 96 and he has to throw back 48.

Throughout your entire reeducation in numbers, it is important to remember that you *do* have the ability, and that the whole process can be *enjoyable* and rewarding.

Logic and Analysis

In a world where communication is becoming increasingly important, and where day after day we are required to "get behind the words" to the truth of the statements from our political leaders, our television and radio, our newspapers and magazines, and our business and scientific advisers, it is essential for all of us to develop our capacity for logical analysis. As propaganda and persuasion techniques have become more sophisticated, so has the mental equipment needed for sorting out the wheat from the chaff. The remainder of this chapter is devoted to ten main areas in which communication can go astray, with examples, explanations of why the communication is not "true," and sections on "how to deal with it."

KEY WORD SUMMARY

Fallacies
Emotional language
Appeal to authority
Undefined source
Changes in definition
Greater good or evil
No decision—no action
Angering the opponent
Yes, but
Biased statistics
Exercises and games

SELF-CHECK 18

A. Circle the term that best describes you as a logical and analytical thinker.

Superior   Excellent   Above average   Average

Below average   Poor   Terrible

B. On a scale of 0–100 (100 = highest) how do you rate yourself as a logical and analytical thinker?

_____

(0–100)

As with creative thinking, the average person assumes himself or herself to be more logical and analytic than the average. Similarly, the scores on the scale of 0–100 average between 60 and 85. As you will now have realized from chapter 7, on creativity, many people underestimate their latent ability. It is the same with logic and analysis, although most people are surprised to find out how very often in their day-to-day lives an enormous amount of illogical and nonanalyzed information sneaks in without their being aware of it at all. As you read this chapter, constantly do a personal check on whether, in advertisements, in the newspaper, in magazines, and in conversations, any of the fallacies outlined here normally get by you.

Fallacies

A logical argument is one in which, if the basic facts or premises are true, the conclusions that follow must be true.

It is usually easy enough to check the facts of any argument by referring to the source, and by asking appropriate questions about the way the facts were established. But do the arguments based on those facts lead to a logical conclusion? This is not so easy to check as it might seem, and many people have been led up the garden path by arguments that appear to be logical but are not.

There are two major forms of logical presentation and misrepresentation, and they can be stated as follows:

1. All As are B
   All Bs are C
   Therefore all As are C

2. All Bs are C
   A is a C
   Therefore A is a B

One of these is correct: the other is not.

A simple diagram of the first example will help us see that if the premise or initial statement is correct, then the final statement will also be correct. If we take the group B, and make it a circle, then the group of As will be a smaller circle within the group of B, because *all* As are B. If all Bs are C, then C will be an even larger circle than B, and as can be seen *all* As will therefore be C.

The soundness of this reasoning can be illustrated by a simple example:

> All ants (A) are insects (B)
> All insects (B) are six-legged (C)
> Therefore all ants (A) are six-legged (C)

Thus this form of argument is correct, *if* the premise is true. If the premise is *un*true this form of argument not only collapses, but often becomes ridiculous, as can be seen from the following example:

> All berries are good to eat
> The deadly nightshade is a berry
> Therefore the deadly nightshade is good to eat

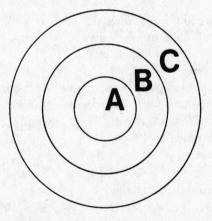

Although this argument is in correct logical form, it is untrue because its first premise is false. So when listening to, or reading, arguments, it is necessary to check that the premises are accurate.

The next thing to check is that the logical form is correct. The second logical form mentioned earlier is an example of an incorrect structure. In the diagram, C once again represents the large group, and because all Bs are C, B can be shown by a smaller circle inside. A is also a C, but A could be either inside the B circle or, significantly, outside it. To reach the final stage of the argument by saying "Therefore A is a B" is to state something that *may* be true, but is not necessarily true. It is therefore a false argument.

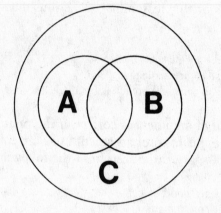

The incorrectness of this form can be seen by an example:

    All mice are four-legged animals
    All elephants are four-legged animals
    Therefore all mice are elephants

This type of argument is quite common in discussions of politics, race, and religion. Forearmed with knowledge of logical structure we can help prevent such discussions from becoming unnecessarily argumentative and unproductive.

The Use of Emotional Language

Emotion in language can be used to the reader's disadvantage or advantage.

It is used to disadvantage when the speaker or writer attempts to color the interpretation of basic facts with his own bias. For example, reporters of political events will often refer to leading politicians in terms which persuade the hearer in one view or another, but which are founded only on personal bias. If the politician is favored, his familiar first name will be used, and the words associated with him will be "positive." The reverse will be done for the politician who is out of favor. For example, "Jim suggests . . ." is far more likely to make us feel pleasantly toward the man than "The Prime Minister demands . . ."

This persuasive use of emotional language can occur even in scientific journals. Experiments that support the work of the writer will be referred to as "elegant," "sophisticated," and "excellent," whereas experiments which are in opposition to the writer's work will be labeled with such emotionally derogative terms as "sloppy," "haphazard," and "ill-conceived."

In any instance where emotional language is used, it is best to listen to the entire message, and then to separate the emotion from the fact.

Emotional language can also be used advantageously, especially in areas such as good prose writing or poetry. In these situations it is the emotion of the language that produces in the reader's mind those images which the writer especially intended to convey to him. To convert such works into pure facts would totally defeat their purpose, as was humorously pointed out by Robert Thouless in his book *Straight and Crooked Thinking.* He used for his example a couplet from the "Eve of St. Agnes," a poem by the English poet John Keats:

> For on this casement shone the wintry moon,
> And threw warm gules on Madeline's fair breast.

Taking the emotion and poetry from these lines, Thouless ended up with the fairly bare and singularly unpoetic lines:

> For on this window shone the wintry moon
> Making red marks on Jane's uncolored chest.

In summary, emotional language can be used both to the reader's advantage and disadvantage, and it is best for him to know *how* the emotion is being used and, just as important, *why.*

Arguments Which Appeal to Authority

Arguments of this sort use the established reputation of a man, a group of men, an organization, or some aspect of the media as "proof" that some thing or some idea must necessarily be true. While such authority is always a useful reference, it can be used only as a *probability* and never, in isolation, as a proof.

Statements such as "Well, I read it in the newspaper, so it *must* be true" or "Well, Professor X, Professor P, Professor Y, and Professor Z all say the same thing as I am saying, therefore I *must* be right" are all too commonly used in both personal and public discussion and debate. The trouble is that even experts and authorities are often at fault.

History has shown that in retrospect virtually every expert has been superseded by someone who had an even wider vision. This itself is enough to warn us of arguments which appeal to authority, as are the frequent instances where two experts on the same subject find themselves in total disagreement.

When faced with such arguments, it is always important to note the authorities being quoted, and then to check *what was said.*

Arguments from an Undefined Source

Arguments of this sort usually assume a solid foundation, but when the argument is looked at more closely, it can be found that there is none.

The source may be *apparently* specific: "experts agree," "reliable sources inform," "someone in a position of authority." Or it may be more general: "everybody knows," "the people of Ireland feel," "it is a commonly accepted fact that . . ."

Each of these arguments is making assertions on bases that are at most weak and may be completely unfounded.

Whenever confronted with such arguments, it is best to pause and ask, "*What* experts?" *Which* reliable sources?" "*Does* everybody know?" and "*Who* says that *all* the people feel?"

A humorous example showing that even the most reliable sources are sometimes at error concerns an Irish finance minister, whose health gave concern to three major European newspapers.

The first reported:

> The budget was delivered by Mr. Lynch, deputizing for Mr. Haughey, in hospital with concussion after hitting his head on a beam earlier yesterday.

The second newspaper was also concerned, and reported:

> Mr. Charles Haughey was knocked unconscious by a piece of gutter which fell from the roof of his house shortly before he was due to make his budget speech today.

A third newspaper completed Mr. Haughey's most unfortunate day:

> Mr. Charles Haughey was taken to hospital after being thrown from a horse only hours before he was due to make his budget speech.

Changes in the Definition of Words

Many communications and discussions become bogged down because subtly and almost imperceptibly the meanings of the key words in the argument change as the argument progresses. This is especially true of discussions revolving around concepts such as "peace" and "good and evil," as well as in discussions about religion, politics, and philosophy.

In such discussions one should of course attempt to define the words. At the same time we have to realize something about the basic nature of words: that rather than having absolute definitions, each word can have hooked onto it a great variety of meanings. Each person will have different associations for each word, and it is therefore important in discussion to find out exactly what meanings the other people in the discussion have hooked on to their key words. People are often surprised to find that in a group it is they and they alone who have given a word certain connections which they had previously assumed to be common.

To bring this point home, it is useful to ask a friend to think of the first six words that in his or her mind connect with words like "run," "God," "happy," and "love," and then compare them with your own first six. The disparity will be both surprising and illuminating. So far in the author's experience no two people have been found who had identical associations for *any* given word!

If this point is allowed for in discussion, far more understanding will develop. The gradual changes in the meanings of the words being used will not be taken so much as evasive or argumentative, but as a natural result of discussion, and one which can be used constructively.

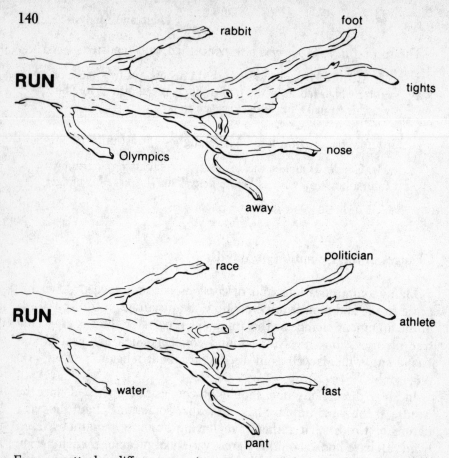

Everyone attaches different meanings to every word, as shown by these two examples from different people of associations for the word "run."

Greater Good or Evil

These arguments usually take the form of "I admit that X is bad, but Y is worse, so there is no point in doing anything about X," or "I admit that X is good, but Y is better, so we may as well forget about X and concentrate on Y."

The dishonesty in these arguments is that they are based on restrictive "either—or" thinking and not on constructive "both—and" thinking. If X and Y are evil, then *both* should be dealt with. And similarly if both X and Y are good, then *both* should be encouraged.

Thus if there is a high crime rate in a city *and* housing conditions are poor, both problems can be dealt with at the same time. And if there is a need for satisfying our curiosity about space *and* a need for better medical facilities, again both can be investigated simultaneously. Even, in those rare instances when only one course of action is possible because of pressure of time, the "both—and" argument still applies. In these instances the most important area is dealt with first *and* the second area is then dealt with as soon as possible.

The "both—and" argument is made even stronger when it is realized that if both activities are engaged in, they usually soon begin to supplement each other. Thus in the first example better housing would automatically begin to reduce crime; and a reduction in crime would tend to lead to a more stable family life.

The investigation of space has already given many benefits to medical science, and medicine in turn has been able to protect the lives of the astronauts.

The No Decision/ No Action Argument

This form of argument arises when there are two equal choices, and where it is exceptionally hard to make a choice between the two. The result is often either inability to decide either way, or an assumption that because the decision is so hard to make there is no point in making it.

It happens surprisingly often in examinations, where many people have a little discussion with themselves over which of two questions to answer, both questions having equal marks. Some students have been known to spend the entire time allowed for the question in trying to decide which one to answer! Similarly, businessmen have been known to spend hours, and even days, shuffling papers and trying desperately to decide where to start. Sometimes they never do.

This situation can normally be clarified by realizing that there are not two choices but three:

1. to take the first option
2. to take the second option
3. to opt out

Looked at in this light, the problem becomes clear and is solved more easily. For the situation that gave rise to the two alternatives is usually one which requires action. If this is the case it can be seen that choice number three is inadequate, and that if the other two choices are so nearly equal it does not really matter which one is chosen, *as long as it is one of them.*

Many people find that in such situations it is useful to flip a coin to decide. There have been reports that having flipped a coin which dictates one choice, they suddenly realize that that really is not the one they want and are thus able to select the other.

The no decision/no action argument is valid only when no action was really desired in the first place.

Angering the Opponent

This technique of arguing, although basically dishonest, is astonishingly successful. The "angerer" finds out things that will especially annoy his opponent and begins to emphasize them, and as a result the opponent, emotionally upset, argues badly.

The answer to this kind of illogical argumentative approach is simply to realize that it is being used. The person who is being emotionally attacked will realize that the "angerer" himself must feel threatened or weak. It is one of the principles of combat that once the person attacked realizes that the attacker is in some way weak or afraid, the attacked person immediately becomes stronger and often assumes the "controlling" role. The same applies to intellectual argument, and it is surprising just how quickly the tables can be turned.

The attacked person can make his counterattack even stronger by realizing how ridiculous the "angerer" is in his attempts at upsetting. He can relax and smile at the irrelevant performance.

The Yes-But Arguments

Many people have been trained to disguise a basically destructive attitude under the initially affirmative "yes" followed by the concealed, contradictory "but." No matter what is answered to the last "but," this person will agree "yes" and then add another "but," and so on. Such arguers are not trying to find the truth of a statement, nor are they trying to extend and expand an idea, but are simply trying to "bring it down."

The way to handle such situations is simply to ask them why they are continually trying to "dampen" the conversation, or ask them, before they can come in with their next "yes, but," to add to and expand the concepts being discussed.

As a general principle it is normally best in conversations to add and expand until a general structure has been built and then to go through with a more analytical eye looking for any possible dangers and faults in the construction.

Arguments Using Biased Statistics

Two newspapers—one favorable to the government in office, the other unfavorable—reported on unemployment.

The first, in a major headline, stated: "Unemployment Total Stays Steady." The first paragraph of the story read as follows:

> Unemployment remained practically static during the past month when the total number of unemployed rose by 3,972 to 601,874 on November 9, representing an unchanged percentage of 2.6.

The other paper used the banner headline: "Unemployed may reach 700,000." Underneath this heading was the lead paragraph.

> Little by little the unemployment figures are creeping up again. This month they have once more topped 600,000, which means they are the worst November total for 30 years.

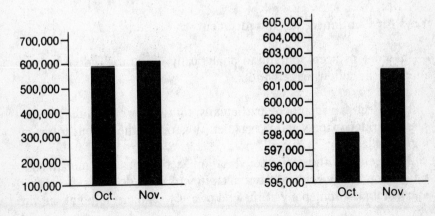

Apart from a large number of logical dishonesties (can you spot them all?) these examples illustrate the selective use of statistics in order to bias the reader toward a certain viewpoint.

In the first article, the newspaper wished to give the impression of stability. All the possible figures were probably analyzed until one was found that showed no change: the percentage.

The newspaper unfavorable to the government likewise found one specific statistic that made the issue look particularly serious.

This example helps to illustrate something more about statistics than the oft-quoted statement that "numbers always lie." It shows that if the reader knows the *ingredients* that go into the statistics presented, he will have a fairly accurate awareness of the situation and will *also* know what bias the presenter of the statistics has.

This approach to statistics makes them far more interesting, for not only do they present numerical information but they also add to the reader's knowledge of the motives behind the presentation of the material.

There are many ways in which figures can be purposely selected and biased, ranging from simple and false assumptions about averages, to the more sophisticated manipulation of graphs to make good situations look bad and bad situations look better than they really are. It is advisable for the reader who wants to get to the "truth behind the numbers" either to take a basic course in statistics or to read some of the more elementary paperbacks on how to interpret the figures that are presented to him. Once the initial fear of statistics and numbers has been overcome, hunting down logical fallacies can be an enjoyable and rewarding pastime.

Keys for Continued Self-Improvement

In order to keep your mind analytically "in trim," adopt one or more of the following activities:

1. Collect in a scrapbook particularly amusing or outstanding examples from newspapers and magazines, illustrating the various forms of logical fallacy.

2. In personal and group conversation "set" yourself to remain continually on the lookout for flaws in argument. This does not necessarily mean stopping somebody at the end of every sentence to point out his

errors, but means keeping a more watchful eye on the trends that conversations take.

3. Occasionally, or continually, examine your own methods of presentation and communication. You will often find the most useful information about your own logical weaknesses during times of extreme anger.

4. If you have a friend or acquaintance who is particularly interested in improving logical and analytical abilities, make a pact to check each other whenever errors occur. This will keep you alert both as presenter of information and as analyst of any information being presented to you.

5. Young children, once they are shown logical fallacies, are often extremely quick to pick them out. Delightful games can be played, scoring if desired, with television and radio newscasts, and with newspapers. Members of the family score points for being the first to recognize logical fallacies in the information they are all absorbing.

6. Buy newspapers and magazines that completely contradict your own viewpoints and compare them with the newspapers and magazines you normally buy.

If these exercises and games are practiced, you will become more confident, relaxed, and communicative with words, and will be more able to deal with the constant barrage of slightly "crooked" thinking with which we are bombarded.

Advice for the Future

You have now completed your first reading of the book, and are ready to plan your continuing mental development for the future. The following are a few items of advice that you may find helpful:

1. Leave this book alone for a few days and then return to it, gently browsing through sections you have read. You have given your mind a few days' rest, which allows it to "digest" the material it has taken in. And you are rereading earlier sections with more complete knowledge than you had when you first read them. So your understanding, comprehension, and appreciation of those sections will be considerably greater than it was the first time, and the number of ideas you will generate for your own personal progress will be that much greater. For example, on reading the section on the right and left sides of the brain a second time through, you will find that all the "hooks" concerning brain patterns, creative thinking, special memory techniques, notemaking, and mathematical ability will connect to the information about the brain, making it far more interesting and relevant than before.

Another thing you might do while browsing through the book is mark off all those sections which give specific advice for exercising and developing your various abilities. This will enable you to refer to the book at any time, immediately selecting those areas in which you wish to give yourself extra practice and strength.

2. Make sure that you start, immediately if possible, to practice developing the fine-tuning of your senses. Practice the exercises recommended in the book and make up your own exercises to develop the natural abilities you possess, not only in seeing and hearing but also in tasting, touching, and feeling.

3. Hold constantly in your mind the knowledge that the development of your mental abilities gets easier the more you attempt it and that after the initial hurdle has been conquered the path is always open to a continuing improvement. No matter where you rate yourself at the moment, if you start even the simplest program of self-improvement, your rewards will be guaranteed.

4. As emphasized in Chapter 2, on memory, review is an essential part of the learning process. Decide which areas you wish to emphasize, and make sure that you have a reasonable program of review, the more automatic the better. The advantage of reviewing, which can't be overemphasized, is that it not only maintains your store of knowledge but also reveals interesting connections, not previously realized, between the various bits of information that you already have in your brain.

5. If possible, organize for yourself a continuing learning plan. This can mean simply going down to the local bookshop or library and obtaining five basic introductory books on a subject that has always interested you and which you have never really given yourself the time to study. It could also mean making the decision to enroll in an adult-education course, in order to give yourself a formal structure in which to learn, as well as a specific goal.

In any such learning plan, make sure that you bring all your mental abilities to bear, motivating yourself throughout to improve not only in the knowledge that you acquire, but also in your abilities to absorb, retain, and use that knowledge.

It is useful, in embarking on such a plan, to organize regular learning periods for yourself. It is also essential to "overview" the subject you will be studying, before you go into greater depth. Rather than simply plunging in and hoping for the best, check on all available sources before starting.

These sources include the specialist magazines and journals that devote themselves to the topic of your particular interest; encyclopedias and reference books, which give excellent overview, and often very useful in-depth treatment; associations and groups brought together because of their interest in the subject which is interesting you; and public information and clipping services, which are usually more than willing to help anyone starting a new area of study.

6. Remember also that your brain is more remarkable than had ever been thought and is very probably more remarkable than we think

even now. The amazing facts about the number of interconnections, the extraordinary retention capacity, and the equal balance of academic and artistic activities have come to light only in recent years.

7. And finally remember that the brain *does* improve with age if it is fed and nurtured properly. No matter what state yours may be in at the moment, the prospect for its future is bright, as long as you decide to make it so.

The best time to make that decision is now.

Further Reading

PSYCHOLOGY / PRACTICAL

Bates, W. H. *Better Eyesight Without Glasses.* Holt, Rinehart & Winston, 1981.
Brown, Mark. *Left Handed—Right Handed.* David S. Charles, 1980.
Buzan, Tony. *Use Both Sides of Your Brain.* E. P. Dutton, 1983.
———. *The Brain User's Guide,* E. P. Dutton, 1982.
Cooper, K. H. *Aerobics.* M. Evans, 1968.
Huxley, Aldous. *The Art of Seeing.* Creative Arts Books, 1982.
Luria, A. *The Mind of a Mnemonist: A Little Book About a Vast Memory.* Contemporary Books, 1927.
———. *The Working Brain.* Basic Books, 1973.
Ornstein, Robert. *The Psychology of Consciousness.* Harcourt Brace, 1977.
Russell, Peter. *The Brain Book.* E. P. Dutton, 1979.
Samuels, M., and Samuels, N. *Seeing with the Mind's Eye.* Random House, 1975.
Steil, Lyman, and Miller, Robert. *Effective Listening.* Telstar, 1982.
Thouless, R. *Straight and Crooked Thinking.* Pan, 1974.

GENERAL READING

Alexander, F. M. *The Alexander Technique.* Thames & Hudson, 1974.
Bergamini, David. *The Universe,* rev. ed. Time-Life Books, 1974.
Gelb, Michael. *Body Learning: An Introduction to the Alexander Technique.* Deliah Books, 1981.
Moroney, M. J. *Facts from Figures.* Penguin, 1951.
Saint-Exupery, Antoine de. *The Little Prince.* Harcourt Brace, 1968.
Scientific American. The Brain. W. H. Freeman, 1979.
Watson, L. *Supernature.* Hodder, 1974.

NOVELS

Herbert, Frank. *Children of Dune.* Berkeley, 1982.
———. *Dune.* Berkeley, 1975.
———. *Dune Messiah.* Berkeley, 1975.
———. *God Emperor of Dune.* Berkeley, 1983.
Hesse, Hermann. *The Glass Bead Game.* Holt, Rinehart & Winston, 1969.
Stapledon, Olaf. *Last and First Men.* Peter Smith.
———. *Odd John and Sirius.* Dover Publications, 1972.
———. *Star Maker.* Peter Smith.
Van Vogt, A. E. *The Players of Null-A.* Berkeley, 1974.
———. *The World of Null-A.* Berkeley, 1982.

Index

abbreviations, in note-making, 108–9
aborigines, 30
addition, 124–28
  complete 10s technique for, 125–26
  multiples technique for, 126–27
  splitting the numbers technique for, 127–28
  10-packet technique for, 124–25
age and aging:
  brain and, 32–33, 149
  hearing and, 63
  listening skills and, 72
  memory and, 37, 56
Ali, Muhammad, 30
analytical observation, 80–83
angering opponents, arguments based on, 142
Anokhin, Pyotr, 25–28, 39
ARCURRC Model, 62, 67–69, 72
argumentation, *see* logic and analysis
Aristotle, 21–22, 87–88, 89
artists, 24–25
Art of Seeing, The (Huxley), 85
assimilation, 68
athletic performance, mind's control over, 30
Augustine, Saint, 89
authority, arguments based on, 137–38
autosuggestion, 31

biased statistics, 143–44
Bidder, George Parker, 53–54
blinking, 84
blood pressure, control of, 29
Bonnet, Charles, 102
boredom, 66
"both-and" arguments, 140–41
brain, 21–34, 148–49
  aging and, 32–33, 149
  combined halves of, 23–24
  connections of, 28
  control of, 29–31

creativity and, 111
electrode stimulation of, 39, 103–4
evolution of, 29
historical views of, 21–22
left vs. right, 22–25, 29, 34, 122
machines vs., 33–34
mathematical calculations by, 122–23
occipital lobe of, 75
potential of, 28–31
self-check for left/right balance of, 34
structure of, 25–28, 111
temporal lobes of, 104
upper and lower, 28–30
brain cells, 25–28
  tentacles of, 27–28
brainspeed, 71
brainstorming, 116–17, 119
brain waves, 23, 29–30
breathing, 84

cerebral cortex, 29
Cézanne, Paul, 25
Christian Church, memory theories of, 88–89
Cicero, 88
color, 23, 56
communication, 69, 72
comprehension, 68
concentration, 63–67
  boredom and, 66
  distractions and, 65–66
  forgetting and, 66–67
conversation:
  argument techniques for, *see* logic and analysis
  memory in, 38
creativity, 110–19
  brain pattern and, 116–17
  brain structure and, 111
  education and, 111–12
  great minds and, 118–19

ABOUT THE AUTHOR

Tony Buzan, psychologist, educator, and poet, is the author of many books on the brain and its functions. He is also the founder of the Learning Method Groups that are given worldwide. He lives in Great Britain.